ADVANCE PRAISE

"This book is a magic wand for creating more in less time. In Idea to Execution, Ari and Nick deliver a brilliant guide for helping entrepreneurs spend more time applying their natural advantages to doing work that truly matters. It's a fascinating read, filled with precise lessons and actionable advice."

— SALLY HOGSHEAD, *NEW YORK TIMES* BEST-SELLING AUTHOR, *FASCINATE*

"Everyone dreams of starting their own business, but only about 1% do it. This book is for the 99% who don't. It walks you through exactly how to test and validate your business idea with minimal risk, and how to scale once it's validated. This is the guide you've been waiting for to stop dreaming and start doing."

— TUCKER MAX, 3X #1 *NEW YORK TIMES* BEST-SELLING AUTHOR, AND COFOUNDER, BOOK IN A BOX

"*Idea to Execution is a fantastic story that all business owners or aspiring entrepreneurs should read in order to stay ahead of the curve. Ari and Nick bring attention to potential issues and how to fix them with elegant solutions. Ari and Nick actually give exact step-by-step answers for how they simplified some of the most complex processes.*"

— JOE POLISH, FOUNDER OF GENIUS NETWORK AND ARTISTS FOR ADDICTS

"*I'm very impressed with the transparency and insights that Ari and Nick reveal in Idea to Execution. They are a perfect example of The Power of Broke and package their journey in a way that is applicable and workable for everyone.*"

— DAYMOND JOHN, FOUNDER OF FUBU AND STAR OF ABC'S *SHARK TANK* (@THESHARKDAYMOND)

"*I have always been focused on highest and best use of time/ effort/talent/opportunity cost/capital (including financial, intellectual, and human). Ari and Nick's new book warp speeds entrepreneurs with limited resources/limited infrastructure from seeming disadvantage into the rarified world of preemptive/masterful/performance AND PROFIT maximum advantage. Great read—IF you are true to your aspiration of wanting to create a meaningful (sustainable) business success.*"

— JAY ABRAHAM, WORLD RENOWNED BUSINESS GROWTH STRATEGIST

IDEA TO EXECUTION

IDEA TO EXECUTION

How to
- OPTIMIZE
- AUTOMATE
- OUTSOURCE

EVERYTHING IN YOUR BUSINESS

ARI MEISEL & NICK SONNENBERG

IDEA TO EXECUTION

How to Optimize, Automate, and Outsource Everything in Your Business

ISBN   978-1-61961-505-2 *Paperback*
       978-1-61961-506-9 *Ebook*

LIONCREST
PUBLISHING

CONTENTS

FOREWORD

———

BY JAY ABRAHAM

Here's the cold, hard truth: you are either *in* control of your business/life/relationships, or *they* control *you*.

Having spent my entire career solving problems and fixing businesses for over ten thousand clients in four hundred different industries, it's easy for me to recognize limiting patterns. From working with business royalty to small business owners, the same problem exists across all categories: *inefficiency.*

Despite existing in a time period where the most sophisticated technology is at our fingertips, many people are finding themselves in the second category. They are controlled in their day-to-day lives by constant distractions, obscure inefficiencies, outdated processes, and other people's demands. You may be in this category yourself, feeling like you are doing far more "doing" than "living." This can send almost anyone into a downward spiral of feeling overwhelmed, stressed, stuck, or emotionally immobilized.

When your happiness hinges on your progress, watching your life become ravenously consumed by your to-do list feels like a slow death. If you are not vigilant with your time, you will easily become reactive to outside urgencies and paralyzed when it comes to the work that actually matters to *you*.

The unawareness of true productivity plagues entrepreneurs in particular. And that's exactly what it is: unawareness. Very few companies know about the capabilities of today's automation tools, and even fewer actually implement these tools. Thousands of hours and dollars are wasted every year by this unawareness, coupled with the lack of proper management of existing systems.

As a business owner, when you tolerate these inefficiencies, they not only impact your income but also your life's purpose. Everyone has a unique genius—something that they are unquestionably "meant" to do.

It may be connecting with people face-to-face, making phone calls, brainstorming and envisioning the future, or uniting teams. Perhaps your gift is revealed in your creative ideas. When you are in this "zone," you know you're doing something right—you gain momentum, you feel fulfilled, your relationships deepen, and your business grows.

But how much time do you spend in that zone every day? If you're like most people, you probably only use about 20 percent of your resource capacity; in other words, your unique gift is being horribly neglected. You've probably heard the phrase, "Do more of what you love," but how is it possible to access the core of this natural power when you are drowning in your own to-do lists?

This is the question everyone's asking. I am proud—and relieved—to say that the answer is finally here.

Ari Meisel and Nick Sonnenberg are two remarkable young men who have made astounding leaps in the fields of optimization, automation, and outsourcing. In addition to helping companies and businesses perform better, they help everyday individuals and entrepreneurs manage stress with some of the most effective techniques I've ever come across in my career.

We have more productivity gurus, apps, education, and support than ever before, and yet simultaneously we have the least amount of credible guidance for how and why we use these assets. Ari and Nick bring a refreshing perspective and insights that will haunt you in the most positive way imaginable.

Now, it may not be your fault that you are overwhelmed, but it is your responsibility. If you are dreaming of having more free time to spend with family, generating more income, and pursuing your personal interests, you simply must learn how to manage and, more importantly, improve your current systems and processes.

This is what we call "optimization."

I've been obsessed with this concept for a very long time. Implementing the most effective use of all your systems is one of the best investments you can make as a human being in modern-day society. If you always seek to improve your use of time, intellect, and people, you will find yourself far ahead of those who settle for "that's just how we do things around here."

And although optimization is a key component, it is just one of the pillars that contribute to a fully engaged, productive process. Ari and Nick have developed an incredibly elegant system that helps people unlock their maximum productivity. It is the king of all systems and pertains to how all systems must be managed: *Optimize, Automate, Outsource.*

After all, what happens after you optimize a process? It can run effectively and have only a couple of steps, but what about other variables that will chip away at your time and energy? While there is still room for human error, your time is still unprotected. That's why the next step is *automation.*

In this masterpiece, you will be introduced to some of the most sophisticated automation tools of our time. Throughout Ari and Nick's inspiring story, you will see how they work to eliminate specific inefficiencies and catalyze productivity. You'll find yourself coming up with ideas and fantasies about automating your own recurring tasks and the relief of never having to touch them again.

Of course, you can optimize all of your systems, automate most, and you may be left with tasks that still require a bit of human touch. But here's the kicker: it doesn't need *your* touch.

Does that offend you?

If it does, you will always be stuck doing more tasks that inhibit your unique genius from being realized. You see, there is nothing more self-limiting than to believe you're the *only one* who can perform a certain task. The truth is all tasks, no matter how complex, follow a specific recipe. If documented in enough detail, anyone can replicate the process and the result. And if someone else can do it, that means *you don't have to*. Instead, you can spend more time using your strengths and with your values.

Take Ari for example. The man has four children, a wife, a dog, manages an entire virtual assistant company and client database, and doesn't work on *anything* that doesn't require his signature touch. This leads to a rich life and thousands of people asking, "How?"

Idea to Execution offers a generous documentation of what the *Optimize, Automate, Outsource* method can do to improve—and actually *build*—an entire business in just one day. You will walk away fully educated about the array of benefits that come from doing less and living more, and learn how to make it work in your own business.

I often see business owners overlooking opportunities, hidden assets (both tangible and intangible), and under-performing in areas that no one else recognizes. The proper use of optimization, automation, and outsourcing tools is rare and underappreciated. It is my honor to introduce you to a robust concept that, when applied, will grant you more time and, most importantly, more freedom.

You will benefit enormously from the transparency and subtle adjustments that Ari and Nick reveal in this thrilling tale. Through recounting the wins and losses of the two resourceful young mavericks, Ari and Nick utilize their own inner geniuses to bring the simplest solutions to the most complex problems—a contribution that will transform thousands of lives, including your own if you read with a compelling purpose to improve yourself or your business.

As you move forward, I invite you to undergo a transformation. Open your mind to the possibility of maximum productivity in your own life. What would that feel like? How would your relationships, your body, your mind, and your life shift? What would you have the freedom to do?

Above all else, are you willing to optimize your own mindset to get there?

If the answer is yes, prosperous and productive times await you.

– JAY ABRAHAM

INTRODUCTION

On a hot summer night in August 2015, financial engineer Nick Sonnenberg and productivity expert Ari Meisel formulated a business while having dinner. They didn't start the meal with the intention of launching a company, but in just a few short hours, that's precisely what had happened. They conceived the company at that table and brought it to life within twenty-four hours.

The two friends shared an interest in the processes of efficiency and productivity—Ari through his "Art of Less Doing" philosophy, books, and coaching program, and Nick through the development of his "Less Planning" scheduling app, Calvin, and his background in algorithmic stock trading.

For years, Ari had been referring his coaching clients to

Zirtual, the largest US-based virtual assistant company. It was backed by Tony Hsieh, the CEO of Zappos. On a random Monday morning in August of 2015, with no warning, Zirtual sent an e-mail to their 2,500 clients and 400 assistants and announced they were shutting down due to financial issues.[1] The message, essentially, was, "Good-bye and good luck."

If anything constitutes breaking news in the productivity world, this was it. Ari's phone started blowing up. Clients and Zirtual employees were in an uproar. People were panicking about their projects, their jobs, and what the hell to do next. In the first few hours of the crisis, Ari scrambled to connect people looking for assistants with the newly unemployed.

Serendipitously, the next night, Tuesday, Nick and Ari got together for a dinner that had been planned weeks in advance. Nick had just returned to New York City from a few weeks in Italy with his girlfriend, Francesca, and Ari's life was in chaos because of the Zirtual explosion. The timing was fortuitous. The two entrepreneurs had long talked about launching a start-up together but had yet to latch onto an idea worth pursuing. Without provocation, an opportunity in the virtual assistant space landed in their laps.

---

1   http://www.businessinsider.com/zirtual-suddenly-laid-off-400-employees-via-email-2015-8

Casually, Nick said to Ari, "Hey, why don't *you* start your own virtual assistant company?" Ari immediately said no. His wife was expecting their fourth child, he'd recently had a falling out with his previous business partner, and he had his hands full running a mastermind group with a group of entrepreneurs. Nick replied, "What if we were partners and did this together?" And Ari gave a snap yes.

During the main course, they started to analyze everything that was wrong in the virtual assistant space and talked about what could be done better. They sketched out what a perfect virtual assistant setup would look like, and the ideas generated from that night have remained the core foundation of the business. Within a day, they built a company.

As a caveat, Ari told Nick he had planned a family vacation the following weekend in Pennsylvania that could not be changed. Even so, they moved quickly. Nick set up all of the initial infrastructure, and Ari secured the first clients before he came back.

They broke a few cardinal rules along the way. Conventional wisdom says you shouldn't go into business with a close friend, but they did it anyway. At dinner, they agreed they would check in with each other periodically, and if the friendship was negatively impacted, they'd stop pursuing the idea.

Despite having a relatively clear picture of what services they wanted to offer and how they would set themselves apart in the market, they never wrote a business plan. Everything happened too quickly for that. It also wasn't necessary. Unlike most start-ups, they didn't have investors to keep happy. They never put together a pitch deck either and took things as they came, without too much planning or forecasting.

Nick and Ari prove that it is possible to build a successful business fast, with zero overhead. They were able to iterate quickly using free tools and apps to launch their company. Growing a scalable, profitable business is within anyone's reach by leveraging people's unique abilities and following the process of Optimize, Automate, Outsource (or OAO). By employing this framework, they were able to minimize errors, reduce costs, and mitigate wasted time.

A full account of Nick and Ari's first year in business is chronicled here: the lessons, the mistakes, the experiments, and, ultimately, the exponential growth. By testing ideas, removing bottlenecks, and leveraging the interaction between humans and technology, the company was both scalable and profitable from day one.

BACKGROUND

—

THE VA LANDSCAPE

A virtual assistant is typically a freelancer who provides remote administrative, technical, or creative assistance. There are two types of virtual assistants available in the marketplace: on demand and dedicated. On demand follows a model in which there is a collection of assistants in a pool. When a request for services is made, any one of those assistants in the pool can complete the task, which is typically a basic assignment that takes about fifteen to twenty minutes. Usually, the tasks are quite straightforward and do not require much explanation or expertise such as making a dinner reservation, doctor's appointment, booking a flight, or buying a gift. They are typically not set up to handle complex tasks.

The other end of the spectrum is the dedicated assistant, which was the model Zirtual followed. In that case, just as it sounds, you work with one specific person consistently. However, dedicated assistants have a greater risk of becoming a bottleneck. They get sick, have car trouble, get fired, or even quit, and then you have to start training someone on your preferences from scratch. Also, from a skill-set perspective, it's unlikely that one person will be able to handle everything you need him or her to do. Maybe the person is great at scheduling appointments, meetings, and travel but not so great at building marketing campaigns, designing websites, or doing market research. Not to mention, one person only has so much bandwidth. If you need one hundred things done, you're going to have to wait a long time for that one person to get to everything.

We already knew from personal experience and from feedback from Ari's clients that there was a *massive* need for a one-stop-shop solution—a system clients can trust to get any job done right. This was a huge advantage for us; we already knew what the market wanted and needed. The most common reason companies fail is because they build something that nobody wants. Not only did we know what the market wanted, but also we had a handful of people willing to pay for it off the bat. The need and value were glaringly obvious.

Back in the day, most of the virtual assistant services were based in India or Pakistan. Those countries offered the cheapest labor source. Low cost used to be a competitive advantage, but like anything, you get what you pay for. Nowadays, the cheapest services are out of the Philippines. However, once you migrate out of the United States, low cost or not, challenges exist when working with a foreign workforce. Cultural and language nuances make effective communication difficult, but some of the international operations still offered great options for off-loading small, low-focus tasks.

A common misconception is that $6/hr is really cheaper than $40/hr. Consider the following: How much is your time worth? First, calculate how much extra time you put into explaining or fixing issues. Let's say your time is worth $60/hr and, on average, it takes you twenty minutes for every hour a VA (virtual assistant) works (time explaining/fixing issues). Effectively, your VA is costing $60/3 = $20 + 6 = $26/hr. Consider the $40/hr person. On average, that person will be 2x–5x faster. For easy math, we'll just say 2x faster. Let's also consider that it will take far less time explaining and fixing mistakes (five minutes per hour). The same task will cost you $40/hr * (½ an hour) = $20 of VA time, and $5 of your time (5 minutes @ $60/hr) = $25. This is a conservative example of the value savings of going with a premium versus basic service. If your time is worth more than $60/hr, it's a no-brainer.

During dinner in July 2015, we identified the pros and cons of the competitors and listed out what the perfect virtual assistant company would look like. For starters, all the VAs would be freelancers paid by the hour (or better yet, by the second). Zirtual made the mistake of hiring all of their VAs as employees. This meant they were paying people to just sit in their chairs and twiddle their thumbs at times. By hiring freelancers and paying by the second, there was no risk to the business. For every hour the VAs logged at $25/hr, we charged the client $40/hr and made, on average, $15/hr.

Instead of charging a flat monthly fee, we wanted people to purchase credits. We also wanted to be fully transparent about how many seconds each task took. This allowed the client to scale up or down with us as needed. The transparency also allowed the clients to monitor how long tasks took, which was something no other company did well. The genius of this was, as a side effect, it provided an extra level of quality assurance.

Second, we wanted to be a hybrid model of dedicated and on-demand assistants. By offering clients a team of assistants, we are able to maintain a level of personalization, while also avoiding the potential bottleneck that having just one person on a task can cause. Third, we wanted to operate at a higher level than the rest of the VA companies out there. We were personally frustrated and disappointed by the quality (or lack thereof) that other services provided.

We wanted to be a one-stop shop, where our clients could get peace of mind. No matter what, we could get the job done in the most efficient way possible. No other VA company at the time was offering large-scale, specialized virtual assistants who could take on any project, and we wanted to capitalize on the opportunity.

OUR BACKSTORY

After an eight-year career as a high-frequency algorithmic trader, Nick was in the process of transitioning from the financial world to the tech sector. He was the founder of CalvinApp, a scheduling and calendar management app. Ari was working with Nick on Calvin as an advisor.

In the summer of 2014, Ari's career took an unexpected turn. He had been coaching individuals on efficiency and productivity strategies for several years. One of his clients (Max), who was in the information-marketing field, approached him with a business proposal. Max had benefited from learning Ari's productivity techniques, and he had some specific ideas about how Ari's coaching business could be expanded. He suggested setting up an elite mastermind-coaching program and hosting a series of quarterly retreats.

Ari went along for the ride, and by the fall, he had transitioned out of private, individualized coaching to concentrate on the mastermind group. Many of his mastermind clients had asked for a training program for their assistants. They saw the impact of the Less Doing methodology on their businesses, and they wanted a way to implement his strategies internally.

In response to the demand for better virtual assistant services, Ari started working on an assistant training program. He found an intern named Kelsey and offered her services to the twelve entrepreneurs within his mastermind group. His plan was to study the types of tasks they asked her to do and work with her on how to best do them.

The people in the test group needed executive assistant-level help, but some of the requests were for specialized projects. Specifically, there was a need for outsourcing management—a single point of contact for any and all project/tasks needs. No one wanted to talk to multiple people about multiple services. They needed a single point of contact for any and all projects, tasks, and needs. At the time, it wasn't clear that this research would eventually become the core of Less Doing Virtual Assistants. The idea for the company hadn't been born yet.

AUGUST

———

CONCEPT TO LAUNCH IN TWENTY-FOUR HOURS

Number of client hours delivered: 26
Number of subscribers: N/A
Revenue: N/A

From day one—or rather, night one, at dinner—we were both strapped for time. Ari had limited brain space to devote to launching a new business, and his hands were full with coaching and speaking engagements. Nick was working full time on his scheduling app, Calvin, which was going to be featured at Twitter's developer conference in October.

EARLY DIFFERENTIATORS

We knew the resources existed to offer a hybrid virtual assistant service with zero investment. The variety and breadth of free technology tools and apps available was staggering, and we intended to capitalize on them.

Before dessert was served, we set about divvying up the tasks necessary to launch our new business. Nick's job was to set up and run infrastructure, and Ari was going to secure the clients, recruit the VAs, and oversee the tasks. Although we were partners, we drew a clear line of responsibilities in the sand. It was understood up front who would be the lead for what. In the early days of any company, everyone needs to wear a million hats and jump in on decisions, but we found that having clear responsibilities helped us to avoid wasted time and unnecessary arguments.

In the beginning, neither of us was sure our idea would become a thriving company. We thought, "Hey, this is a cool idea. Let's try it. It'll be fun." Our decision to give it a try was based on the thinking that, worst-case scenario, we would learn a lot by working with each other. Personal growth is really important, but many CEOs are focused entirely on the money. Picking a partner we could both learn from was one of the early keys to our success. No matter what happened, we'd be winners. When you're learning, you're growing, and the money usually follows.

A lot of start-ups fail because they don't get their systems and assumptions set up correctly to begin with. They waste time and resources circling back, trying to undo early mistakes. We were able to set up the business in an efficient manner because we started with the right business model and the right technology. We never had to go back and undo costly early errors, and we invested zero dollars into getting the company up and running. As experts in efficiency tools and apps, we used off-the-shelf tools rather than developing a custom solution, and we are still using those tools to this day.

Within twenty-four hours, Ari secured clients and Nick created an infrastructure for managing tasks and tracking time (all with free tools). Ari left town for vacation with his family, while Nick and Kelsey, our executive assistant from the mastermind group, handled the tasks that came in. For the first month or so, we performed tasks for the clients under an alias name. This experience allowed us to understand what clients wanted and how to best communicate with them.

TECH TOOLS

The first tool we set up was Trello, the free project management software, which we used to manage client tasks. Trello is
a visual task/project management tool broken up by boards
(projects), lists (statuses), and cards (tasks). Typically, lists
follow a kanban style, which represent various phases a task
might move through: backlog, doing, or done.

Like most tools, we didn't use Trello as traditionally intended.
Each board is treated as a client, and we created preset lists
in all of the boards for consistency. By doing this, we saved
a ton of money because we didn't have to create a custom
website and app for managing the clients' tasks. Not to mention, many of our clients already used Trello, so we spent a
limited amount of time educating them. Clients were quickly
up and running when we invited them to their Trello board
and had them download the Trello app.

Time tracking was another immediate necessity. We set up Toggl, a free time-tracking tool, to log time by the second for each task. Also, Toggl automatically creates itemized reports, which we shared with the clients for full transparency.

Next was Slack, the free messaging app, for internal communication. From the very beginning, we were a zero e-mail company. We set up further integration through Zapier and IFTTT, both app automation tools and also both free. These tools enable you to automate the kinds of actions that take thirty to sixty seconds to complete, but you do them dozens or hundreds of times a day. You can start with things as simple as "IF I update my profile picture on Facebook, THEN update my profile picture on Twitter" or, "IF someone buys something from me on PayPal, THEN add them to my mailing list on MailChimp." The automations can be strung together to complete complex actions such as the creation of an entire podcast production or even the hiring process.

Honestly, it doesn't really matter what your business idea is. We discovered that any idea could be tested and validated quickly, without extensive investment or development. Rather than spending six to nine months developing a perfect app for our services, we tested our systems on a small group of clients. We examined how they used it, what they liked, and what they didn't, and it cost nothing.

From day one, we committed to accepting any request or task, no matter how small or large, as long as it was legal. The way we looked at the business in the beginning, and the way we continue to look at it today, is as one extended experiment. We've been successful using this approach. It has allowed us to quickly assess the results and pivot when necessary.

When the Less Doing Virtual Assistants idea was born, we discussed the lack of high-quality virtual assistants, and we wanted to change that. One of our immediate differentiators was the fact that we only worked with highly trained and capable VAs. In order to attract and retain such a workforce, we decided to pay them a significantly higher rate than the industry standard (roughly two to six times the average). We also wanted to work exclusively with top-tier clients and their businesses and decided, in turn, to charge them four to eight times more than other virtual assistant companies in our space.

THE SERVICE

We saw our services as the antidote to procrastination. We designed the company so that clients could hand over their entire to-do lists to us. In this way, we're also the antidote to stress, because people have more control over their lives when they outsource. A lot of our clients felt they didn't have the time, the money, or the bandwidth to get everything they needed to do done. We solved their problems, both personal and professional.

On the business end of the spectrum, someone might come to us and know they need to implement a sales funnel. They have no clue how to go about creating one or who to consult. We take care of it. If someone has an idea for an app, but doesn't know how to go about sourcing developers or designers, no problem: we've got it. We build the app, the website, and the social media marketing campaign to accompany it. We can even service the app with our own people for the customer service component. Our clients simply give us their ideas, and we do everything else.

For example, our friend, client, and early adopter, Chip, owns a real estate company. We devised a system for him in which we manage all of his business leads, which come through a website we helped him build. When a lead comes in, one of our VAs follows up on it. If the lead is qualified, a VA books an appointment. All that Chip's brokers need to do is show up. We serve as the back-end system for his entire business.

In a nutshell, we help people achieve their goals. We allow them to focus on their unique abilities while we take care of the rest. It is our deep belief that people should work on only the things they derive true enjoyment from, or that they have a comparative advantage in. We're idealists and believe that if people can off-load some of their stress and focus on what matters to them, the world will inherently be a better place.

For example, a high-level executive should not sit on hold for thirty minutes with customer service. That's not a good use of his or her time. That person would be more effective focusing on a higher-priority task. We help people get rid of the time sucks and the junk that zaps them of energy and creativity. We allow them to do things they never thought they had time to do before.

Some of the earliest services we provided for businesses included podcast creation, social media management, and custom dashboards. We made podcast production super easy. All the clients need to do is record their message, and we'll do everything else: editing, design, and distribution. For social media, we create strategies, content, fan pages and more. Custom dashboards allow companies insight into performance and helps identify where there might be bottlenecks. We even created an internal dashboard for the publisher of the book you're reading (Book In A Box).

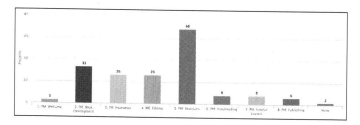

This snapshot allows the company to easily spot where there are jam-ups in their process and address them accordingly.

We also created a dashboard to track revenue:

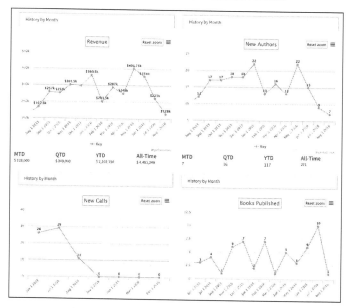

Another area we found clients needed help was with travel arrangements. Because we know our clients' personal preferences and have a system to keep track of everyone, they find it's faster and easier for us to book flights, hotels, and cars on their behalf. Whether they need a quick business trip to Cleveland or are planning a month-long vacation to the Galapagos Islands, we offer full service and handle all of the necessary arrangements.

Basically, we started to pay attention to all of the tiny little things in life that annoy us, take up too much time, or that we just don't want to hassle with. For example, we were on a flight on the way to a meeting. The Wi-Fi on the plane wasn't working. This may sound like a trivial matter, but we were both planning on working on the flight. Three hours of time is a precious commodity, and we were highly irritated at the prospect of losing it. Most people in a similar situation would feel bothered and then pick up a magazine and forget about it.

We took a screenshot of the Wi-Fi error message and sent it to one of our VAs when we landed. We asked her to see what she could do about the problem and wound up getting a $50 credit from the airline. We weren't able to recoup the lost hours, but we were happy to have been compensated for the inconvenience.

There is a huge mental component to off-loading and outsourcing tasks. We wanted to tap into the relief that comes from unloading your annoying to-do list and the satisfaction of pursuing a worthy idea. So many people just don't have the time to pursue their passion. We help them execute on their ideas, which is a highly gratifying endeavor.

Our clients often use our services for personal tasks, which we strongly encourage. Ari used one of our VAs to sign three of his kids up for summer camp because he knew it would save him a ton of time. Just getting them enrolled required applications, payments, doctor's appointments, and vaccinations—times three. The VA even marked the days and times the kids were in camp on Ari's and his wife's calendars so they could stay on top of everything.

Travel disasters are almost inevitable these days. Nick's luggage was lost on a recent trip to Iceland. One of our VAs booked the complete itinerary, but when his bag was lost on the way home, another VA stepped in, located the luggage, and even got him a $250 credit with the airline. She also took the liberty of finding him the best luggage-tracking device on the market (Trakdot) so he wouldn't be inconvenienced again. We use our VAs for personal and internal tasks all the time including screening new hires, payroll, and design development.

People use VAs to keep their fridge stocked, pay the household bills, pick up dry cleaning, buy dog food, plan family travel, process health insurance claims, schedule appointments, complete school paperwork, you name it.

We were only interested in hiring high-quality people we could quickly train in our Less Doing methodology of Optimize, Automate, and Outsource (or OAO). Our process was developed through extensive early research and experimentation. We designed a system to help people become exponentially more efficient by optimizing their time and energy, automating the majority of their day-to-day tasks, and outsourcing everything they didn't need to be directly involved in. OAO is at the core of everything we do to help our clients do less and live more.

BUILDING THE TEAM

Number of client hours delivered: 96
Number of subscribers: N/A
Revenue: N/A

THE HIRING AND ONBOARDING PROCESSES

In September, we focused on hiring top-level virtual assistants. We knew that screening and interviewing candidates would be a time suck, and we didn't want to waste a lot of time going back and forth e-mailing with candidates to schedule a time for an interview. We set up Google apps for business and created e-mail accounts and aliases (va@lessdoing.com, jobs@lessdoing.com, interview@lessdoing.com). All applicants received an auto-response with specific instructions on how to apply.

This system allowed us to quickly scan through applicants and considerably narrow the pool without wasting any of our own time. The bigger genius and added bonus behind screening applicants this way is that it was the simplest possible filter for VAs. If they couldn't figure out how to upload a video and e-mail us a link to YouTube, they'd never cut it as a VA with us. We eliminated over 80 percent of the applicants before we invested a single minute of our time. This is a perfect example of the first step in the Less Doing philosophy: "optimize." Without much technical setup, we optimized the hiring process.

For the video, we simply asked the applicants to tell us about themselves. We were interested to see what type of information they felt was relevant or interesting about them. You can learn more about someone in a two-minute video clip than you ever could through a cover letter or a resume. In fact, we never looked at resumes. The video was all we needed.

Because of our previous research, and what we knew based on feedback from the mastermind group, we wanted to find people with a unique combination of capabilities. We weren't completely focused on finding specialists at the beginning. Rather, we approached our staffing search with the intention of finding and training generalists.

We were looking for a few specific characteristics. Most of which cannot be trained or learned. Most importantly, we wanted all of our VAs to possess a proactive mind-set. You either have it or you don't. For example, one of our VAs noticed that a client was partial to a certain brand of whiskey on a Facebook post. The VA made a note in the client's file, and when his birthday came around, we sent over a bottle. That level of attention to detail demonstrates that the person is thinking ahead, anticipating, and planning ways to go above and beyond expectations.

We wanted our VAs to be more like relationship managers than technically skilled workers. We were also drawn to people who had the attitude that whatever the task or assignment, they would figure it out and wouldn't take no for an answer. If the answer or the solution wasn't immediately apparent, they would hunt through all of the available resources until a solution was found. They would not go back to the client and say it can't be done. They would have a client-centric approach to all of their interactions and communicate professionally. Essentially, we were looking for people who paid attention to detail and who wanted to create the best possible experience for our clients.

We had a client one time who wanted a baby monitor repaired. The VA tried the traditional route of fixing the problem by contacting the manufacturer. The company that made the monitor had stopped producing that particular model and couldn't help. Instead of telling the client he was out of luck, the VA came up with a crafty solution. She suggested the client use Sugru, an air-drying rubber compound, in order to fix the monitor, and the problem was solved.

Video applications revealed these attitudes very quickly. If someone's video was only thirty seconds long, he or she was not utilizing the time allotted to make an impression. Similarly, if someone's video ran eight minutes long, he or she clearly could not follow the most basic directions. Video also showcased the applicant's personality. Usually, 20 percent of applicants didn't make it simply because they seemed awkward or uncomfortable in their own skin.

We needed people who were confident and eager to help. We were not a traditional VA company just ticking off tasks; we were offering long-term solutions. It's a two-way street. Another huge benefit of the video application was the time saved by not having to go back and forth trying to find a time to meet. The goal was to keep things asynchronous whenever possible.

If the video was good, then applicants were required to complete sixteen hours of training on Lesson.ly, an online platform for customizing quizzes. They were tested on their knowledge and needed to score > 90 percent. If this was successful, they took a critical thinking test administered by HireSelect, which measures core competencies as well as predicted levels of conscientiousness and pride in their work. Next was a background check through a tool called Checkr, and then they were sent legal documents via Hellosign to digitally execute. This process was fully automated through a tool called Intuit Workforce.

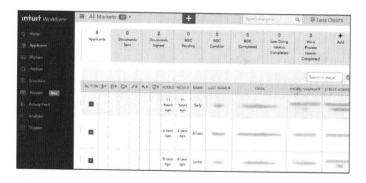

Applicants advanced or dropped off automatically based on how they did at each step. At no time did we ever speak with the applicants on the phone or in person.

Once they were hired, they were automatically added to Toggl, Trello, and Slack. We had a weekly video call with everyone on Mondays using a web conferencing tool called Zoom, which is the first opportunity we had for a face-to-face, or screen-to-face, conversations. We found Zoom to be the best tool for web conferencing. It's the most stable, especially if you are speaking with people in China.

We both have strong intuition when it comes to knowing if someone is going to work out or not. Our requirements are specific and immediately identifiable. Occasionally, someone slips through the cracks, but more often than not, one of us says, I don't think John is going to cut it. Invariably, that person won't be around for too long. It's better for us and better for the candidate to move on swiftly. We have always had the mind-set to hire fast and fire faster.

PRICING

After just a few weeks of being open for business, we added monthly subscription-based fees on top of the hourly rates our clients were already paying. We didn't want them to lose momentum and stop using us. Through subscriptions, we thought we could avoid having a bunch of inactive clients. The monthly fee structure was a big key to our eventual long-term success. Having a steady revenue stream made it easier to budget and forecast.

TECH TOOLS

Once we started to build our team, our clients' security became an important priority. VAs typically handle a lot of sensitive, personal information. We wanted to ensure our clients' privacy and protect their financial records, passwords, and identities. To that end, we set up LastPass, the password management tool, to make sure the clients' confidential information was secure.

LastPass was one of many examples, like Trello, where we used the service in a way the company had never even considered before. We set it up so that clients could share their passwords with us in a secure way, and we just had access to their accounts without ever seeing their passwords. We basically hacked their program to solve our needs.

Initially, we offered two levels of service: premium and standard. Aside from the financial difference, a standard subscription guaranteed a seventy-two-hour response time, whereas the premium promised a twenty-four-hour turnaround. Looking back, it's crazy to us that anyone would be okay with seventy-two hours. At that time, the majority of the clients were on the premium plan.

The standard plan was almost like training wheels for working with us. We didn't expect too many people to stay with it. The idea was that once they got on the standard plan and experienced our capabilities, they would upgrade to premium. Eventually, we dropped the standard plan because we wanted signing up to be as simple as possible. We saw the benefit the premium plan gave existing clients, and we wanted to motivate the least active clients to dig deeper and see the changes the services could make for them.

Initially, our primary focus was simply to sign up more clients. We weren't concerned with metrics or measurements of any kind, aside from how many billable hours we were logging each week. Our aim was straightforward: to provide the most efficient and reliable virtual assistant services on the market, which remains our focus today. More clients meant more requests, which gave us the motivation to know more, stay sharp, be responsive, and keep momentum.

3

OCTOBER

GENIUS NETWORK

Number of client hours delivered: 187
Number of subscribers: 53
Revenue: $26,000

ACCIDENTAL SUCCESS

In June of 2013, Ari was invited to speak at the exclusive Genius Network Event (aka, the $25K Group) in Arizona. Joe Polish, the marketing expert, is the founder of the event. It is the premier conference for high-achieving individuals to connect and collaborate. The invitation came as a complete surprise. Ari answered an unrecognized FaceTime video call, and the person on the other end was Polish, someone Ari was unfamiliar with at the time.

Polish had learned about Ari through David Bach, author of *The Automatic Millionaire*, which was a number-one *New York Times* best seller for thirty-one weeks. Bach had been a client of Ari's and provided the testimonial on his first book cover for *Less Doing, More Living*. He had nothing but good things to say about the "Optimize, Automate, and Outsource" process.

When Polish called, he had already been through Ari's book and diligently highlighted the areas that resonated with him. He said, "I'm here with David, and I've just read your book." He held the marked up copy to the camera to prove it. "You have got to come speak at my event next month." Ari readily agreed.

Speaking at the Genius Networking event in 2013 was the best thing Ari could have done for his career, his first book, and his personal exposure to some of the best and brightest minds in the country. Joe and Ari formed a friendship at the event and eventually Ari worked informally with Joe to improve his own productivity. Ari signed up for the event in the years that followed, and he had it on the calendar for October 2015, months before we came up with the idea for our virtual assistant business.

A few weeks before the 2015 event, Ari told Joe what he and Nick were working on. Their idea was met with great enthusiasm. Joe asked if they would like to do a workshop on the topic of outsourcing on the third day of the event. He even offered them a sponsor booth for maximum exposure. Ari hung up the phone with Joe, called Nick, and said, "Pack your bags. We're going to Arizona."

The Genius Network attracts some of the biggest names in the entrepreneurial business world, and 2015 was no different. The speaking roster was a veritable who's who of industry titans, best-selling authors, and serious power players.

For the first two days, we manned the booth and talked to everyone who approached us. The response was extremely positive; we signed up a few new clients, and we felt energized just being in the room with the top-tier talent. Our friend Nir, the author of *Hooked: How to Build Habit-Forming Products*, even told us we had a knockdown winner on our hands. We were pumped.

Prior to the event, Joe and his team promoted our outsourcing workshop to the event's attendees. They sent a teaser video[2] of our concept around, and the response was fantastic. A few people even changed their flights to stay an extra day and see us. At the time of the event, we had about thirty people signed up to participate.

2   https://lessdoists.wistia.com/medias/43yinn2tj9

On the second day of the conference, Ari got up on stage—which had just been warmed up by Tony Robbins and Peter Diamandis—and directed people to our booth. He plugged our workshop and even more people changed their flights to stay and see us. Momentum picked up, and by day three, we had seventy people enrolled for our workshop.

We had no agenda for our presentation. There was no PowerPoint or any structure planned for what we wanted to say. We had a poorly designed logo, a hard to pronounce business name, and a loose idea of what we wanted to cover. There was a brief, preliminary discussion about who would cover what, and we decided that the best way to educate the group was to show them the tools we used and how we used them. There we were, in a room full of the world's most driven people—easily over a billion dollars of combined net worth—unscripted and on the fly.

We stood up in front of this group of extraordinarily high-level and demanding individuals and proclaimed that we could do anything. We took the bold road and ended up presenting for close to three-and-a-half hours. Ari talked about the importance of tracking behaviors and simply knowing where time is being wasted, or, more accurately, not used productively. Nick highlighted the options available for outsourcing any number of tasks and demonstrated the simplicity of each application. The critical point was that no matter how much success the people in the audience had, time was the one thing they couldn't buy more of. We'd identified ways to make it feel like they could buy time by streamlining it as effectively as possible.

We showed them how we use Trello and Slack, Toggl and LastPass. People asked great questions, and, happily, it was an interactive discussion. Real problems were posed, and we had immediate, quantifiable solutions.

In our minds, we weren't pitching our services. We were simply showing the people in the room what was possible with outsourcing and how we built our company with free tools in just a day. It wasn't until they started to ask questions about their specific needs that we found ourselves responding affirmatively. "Yes, we can do that. Sure, we'll show you how. Are you familiar with this tool? It's free. Here's how it works." We demonstrated integration capabilities, communication options, and overall solutions across multiple efficiency channels.

By the end of the workshop, 90 percent of the room signed up to use our service, and a handful inquired about private consulting. At that time, we only had about twenty clients, and they were all people we knew in some capacity.

Suddenly, we were moving into a new realm and working with people once or twice removed.

Working with upper-echelon clientele held our services to a higher standard. These types of people give harsh and immediate feedback when something isn't working out to their satisfaction, and it kept us on our toes. Right away, we had our reputation to protect. In fact, Joe made it known that he took vouching for us very seriously.

The feedback we received was simply phenomenal. Multiple people told us our presentation was the best one of the entire event. The day after the workshop, we sat down with Joe to recap. He was as fired up about the response as we were, and it was decided that he would become a partner in the company.

GETTING REAL

Our heads were spinning. The true potential of our idea really clicked for us at the Genius event. This was no longer some fun, let's-see-if-it-works, side-hustle project. We had each been spending about ten hours a week working on the business, but after the event, we realized we were onto something big. We were both going to have to up the ante and devote considerably more time to the company.

Behind the scenes in those early days, we were both heavily involved with the tasks and were still figuring out the best and most efficient ways of getting things done for clients. Like all entrepreneurs, we needed to be very hands on in the beginning. We were learning best practices so that we could then train incoming staff and have a better sense of the skill sets we needed in new hirers. In order to really understand our business, we needed to be familiar with every single job and what it involved, from the lowest to the highest level. During August and September, we were able to cull that vital information by doing it ourselves. There was a huge benefit for us, not only in seeing the kinds of tasks clients needed help with but also becoming familiar with *how* they communicated their needs. We needed to know if a VA would be able to understand fully the intent of what a client was asking for and respond to it properly. We also needed to understand the psychology of the work we would hire people to do.

Prior to the Genius event, we began the process of recruiting and retaining the highest caliber people to work for us. Because we wanted the best of the best, we came up with a few ways to incentivize high performing VAs. We implemented $100 weekly bonuses for the person who did the best job. Bonuses were granted based on things that were important to us such as availability or responsiveness. Sometimes bonuses were awarded because of positive client feedback or sharing a good idea on Slack.

Our measurement system at the time was entirely subjective. In addition, the VAs who really showed pride in their work were given the most interesting tasks and more complex projects. The intellectual stimulation of the work was part of their incentive.

We also started offering five hours of paid training a month in any area the VA was interested. It could be anything from e-mail marketing to wood carving. The intention was to hire people who had a constant thirst for learning and the desire to keep improving. The VAs took us up on this training and usually chose a topic that was directly relevant to their work.

Another incentive was the opportunity to work with us directly: two highly regarded productivity experts, which carried a lot of value for people in this space. We were able to provide new hires with an incredible educational experience, so people interested in learning were given the opportunity for specialized industry knowledge.

October was a busy month of hiring, but just as swiftly, we immediately fired people who were not working out. Our systems were set up in such a way that it was very easy to remove someone. All we needed to do was remove them from LastPass, Trello, Toggl, and Slack. It literally only took one minute.

TECH TOOLS

Prior to the event, we'd been using a payment processor that required us to input all of the credit card information manually, which was bad from both security and productivity perspectives. While manning the booth of Genius Network, we made the decision to switch to Stripe as our payment processor, which was a vast improvement. While we were on a flight home from Arizona, we imported all of the new clients from the Genius Event into the system and charged sixty new clients the equivalent of $25,000 in just a few hours.

Later in the month, we took payment processing to the next level and set up Chargify as the front-end payment portal, while still using Stripe as a processor. A very simple subscription billing software, Chargify eliminated the need to enter any information manually, which was about to become cumbersome with the volume of business we anticipated.

Chargify also has a wide variety of capabilities you don't know you need until you need them, such as dealing with expired credit cards by notifying the client automatically. It allowed us to upgrade, downgrade, or cancel a client's subscription easily. There was a self-service page, which allowed clients to update information on their own. It provided metrics month over month on critical data such as the number of customers, revenue, and lifetime client value. It also protected us because it only allowed us to see the last four digits of someone's credit card, so it killed several birds with one stone.

Revenue Performance

Bootcamp	Last Month	This Month
BPO 5hr Consulting	$2,500	$2,500
LDBootcamp47	$564	$423
Coaching	**Last Month**	**This Month**
3 Month Recurring	$0	$0
3 Month	$0	$0
Coach Certification	$0	$30,000
Dummy	**Last Month**	**This Month**
VA	**Last Month**	**This Month**
$1	$6	$3,153
STANDARD25	$615	$825
AdditionalBoard	$0	$150
PREMIUM99	$19,077	$15,643
PREMIUM129	$45,010	$46,305
PREMIUM149	-$20	$1,043
PREMIUM349	$0	$0
Biz Bootcamp	$0	$0
Annual Discount Plan	$5,289	$5,794
BPO_1500	$0	$0
Annual Plan	$0	$0
Workshop	$0	$0
STANDARD10	$820	$20
Totals	**$73,860**	**$105,855**

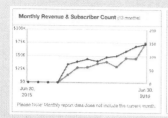
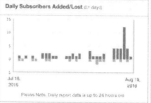

Additionally, Chargify integrated beautifully with the automation tools we were already using, specifically Zapier, Trello, Toggl, Google, and MailChimp. Chargify became the trigger for all Zapier automations.

For example, when someone signed up in Chargify, it triggered the creation of a Toggl project and a Trello board. The person was added to our weekly newsletter list through MailChimp and removed from another MailChimp list for people on a waiting list to use the service. Finally, the person received a welcome e-mail directly from our Gmail account with instructions on how to use Trello along with a digital copy of *Less Doing, More Living*.

We still had to do a few things manually, but overall we saw efficiency improvements right away. From the beginning, we invested time in the initial setup of our systems, so we could focus on more important things.

On a personal level, the trip to Genius Network marked the end of Ari's mastermind coaching program. He also made the decision not to book anymore speaking engagements for a year, in part because of what was happening with the company but also because of his family commitments. Without the mastermind group or a packed calendar, Ari had more time to focus on growing the business.

Nick's app, Calvin, was featured at the Twitter developer conference the same month, just before we went to Genius in Arizona. He had been out in San Francisco working around the clock with his developers, who he had flown in from Bulgaria, Switzerland, China, and San Diego. They were pushing hard to get Calvin into the app store prior to the Twitter convention. He even had one of our VAs look into how to expedite an app review. Calvin had been his top priority for years, and it was on the verge of launching.

Point being, we had both been running hard in our respective areas of focus, but Genius changed all of that. We had to slow down, reassess, and conscientiously admit that the company had real potential. It was going to need more of our time. It was a huge turning point for us, both personally and as business partners. Although neither one of us had ever expected it to take off, suddenly, we were in orbit.

4

NOVEMBER

GROWTH SPURT

Number of client hours delivered: 585
Number of subscribers: 68
Revenue: $14,500

SCALABILITY

The Genius Network Event changed the scope of our individual and collective focus. We were fortunate to sign up so many new clients and very lucky that only a few of them started using us right away. We were given a few weeks of grace time to get our ducks in a row before being inundated by an influx of task requests. Most of the people who signed up wanted to get in on the ground floor at a discounted rate, but it was a little while before they transitioned into active clients.

The downtime gave us the breathing room we needed to realize we weren't set up to be sustainable for the long run. Nick was concerned that if a large volume of clients came on board, we weren't going to be able to handle everyone efficiently. He thought we needed a better solution to know what tasks to prioritize.

Nick got to work on the first version of a dashboard, which he coded in a language called Python. He ran the script, took a screenshot of it, and posted it to Ari in Slack. Here's an example:

The script basically aggregated all of the Trello cards, which were tasks from clients, and prioritized the tasks so that the VAs would know where they needed to focus their attention first. Nick recognized that if we were going to scale, we needed the dashboard to be able to prioritize.

The brilliance of Trello was that we didn't have to build an app from scratch to fit our needs; we just used their platform. Each client had the same preset lists, so we were able to see the whole picture in one place. Because of the wide variance and complexity within the tasks we were asked to do—everything from making a dinner reservation to building a website—we couldn't measure our progress based on completion time.

A better metric for us was the time since the last comment on a task, which was a metric we could compare across all tasks no matter how complex. We decided that no matter what the task, there should be some standard of frequency with which we updated the clients. We started to keep track of the time since the last communication and were able to update our dashboard from oldest to newest. This change helped us to prioritize tasks and spot potential issues before the client complained.

A lot of the implementations and optimizations we made during the third month were both technological and psychological. After Nick created the dashboard, we had a better understanding of what we were looking at and when tasks came in. In fact, our whole approach to tasks changed. We had encouraged the VAs to pick up projects as fast as they could, even if it took them a day or more to start the task. They notified the client that the task had been received, and they started working on it.

The dashboard highlighted some of the problems behind this practice. With a small team, all of a sudden each VA was working on twenty or more tasks at a time. It quickly became very difficult to manage. Delays popped up, and it was hard to get a response from people on specific tasks. We made an adjustment so that the VAs only picked up a task when they had the time to focus on it and complete it. This was an important shift in the way we looked at tasks and the way we managed expectations too.

PIVOTING

In November, Ari handled the clients, customer service, and the internal team. Nick dealt with the finances, business logistics, and technology. Like any new business, not all of the changes we made were positive. To the credit of our setup and the strength of our systems, we were able to reverse very quickly out of a bad idea, which we had to do on several occasions.

One of our bad ideas was to set up pod leaders. As the team grew, we divided them into groups and appointed three senior VAs to lead each group. We were borrowing from a structure Zirtual had used. Within four days, it started to look like a terrible idea. We took people with no management experience whatsoever and tried to turn them into managers, which didn't work.

One of the pod leaders was so focused on being positive and cheerful that nothing was getting accomplished. She wanted everyone on her team to be happy, but the tasks fell by the wayside. Another one of the pod leaders made no changes whatsoever to her team. She basically said they're doing what they need to do. I'm not going to get in their way. The third pod leader fell somewhere in the middle of the other two extremes. After just a few days, we scrapped the idea.

We've been known to throw people into the deep end and see what they are capable of, but in this particular case, it was a mistake. We should have been clearer about expectations upfront so people were set up to succeed instead of struggle. Since then, we implemented the Fascinate personality test[3] to our VA onboarding process. The results helped everyone have a better understanding of how to work well together and where their individual strengths lie.

By mid-month, our hiring process was streamlined beautifully. In fact, we still use the same systems and process today as we did back then. In the early days, we did a lot of post-hiring training. The problem was new hires didn't understand why we did things the way we did them.

3   http://www.howtofascinate.com/our-mission

Incoming VAs were presented with a ton of information, and we started to lose people. We needed a system that could take them through the various phases of being vetted, educated, and brought up to speed *before* they were hired.

The deeper into the business we got, the better we became at automating. It's in our DNA to always look for the best and fastest ways to do things, and we have always tested our services first. To keep our clients engaged, we rolled out a weekly webinar and newsletter on outsourcing. The idea was to feed our clients resources so they could learn about the value of outsourcing.

TECH TOOLS

We attended a conference and learned about a great back-ground-checking tool called, appropriately enough, Checkr. Checkr happened to have integration with Intuit Workforce, which is an incredible resource for companies that have virtual staff as we do.

Intuit is a huge company, but right off the bat, our contact over there was highly responsive and willing to customize the service to suit our needs. Anytime a new VA was brought on board, they had to fill out a W-9 and sign a nondisclosure agreement, provide us with a bunch of information for payroll, and complete a pile of other paperwork we didn't want to chase around.

Aside from saving a huge amount of time, Intuit was equally as valuable as an error-proofing system. There were so many steps in our hiring process, all of which built on each other, and we were getting frustrated. Our Intuit contact worked with us to create a system where one action triggered another, so we didn't have to think about it. We use it for the entire hiring and onboarding process, including all of the paperwork, the background check, and the education component.

HIRING PROCESS

Potential hires go to
www.workforlessdoing.com

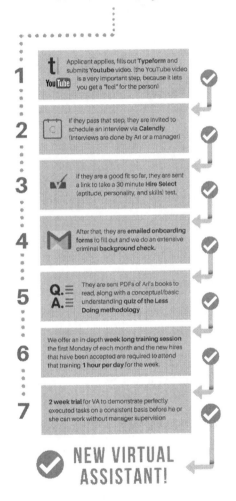

1 Applicant applies, fills out **Typeform** and submits **Youtube** video. (the YouTube video is a very important step, because it lets you get a "feel" for the person)

2 If they pass that step, they are invited to schedule an interview via **Calendly** (interviews are done by Ari or a manager)

3 If they are a good fit so far, they are sent a link to take a 30 minute **Hire Select** (aptitude, personality, and skills) test.

4 After that, they are **emailed onboarding forms** to fill out and we do an extensive criminal **background check.**

5 They are sent PDFs of Ari's books to read, along with a conceptual/basic understanding **quiz of the Less Doing** methodology

6 We offer an in-depth **week long training session** the first Monday of each month and the new hires that have been accepted are required to attend that training **1 hour per day** for the week.

7 **2 week trial** for VA to demonstrate perfectly executed tasks on a consistent basis before he or she can work without manager supervision

NEW VIRTUAL ASSISTANT!

5

DECEMBER

GROWING PAINS

Number of client hours delivered: 1,033
Number of subscribers: 78
Revenue: $28,000

CHALLENGES AND OBSTACLES

Four months into the company, we were still experimenting with efficiencies and systems to see what worked the best. We started a monthly client survey to tailor our services to their feedback. Like most surveys, however, the response rate was low at about 5 percent, which was disappointing. One benefit of the survey though was that it showed us we weren't engaging with our clients properly. People who had enrolled were not using the service as often or as effectively as they could have been, and we also saw low engagement in the weekly webinar we rolled out the previous month.

At one point, we thought having an office might help improve team communication and culture. We wanted to create a strong culture and give the VAs an opportunity to work with us directly. One of the incentives for them has always been the Less Doing education that working for us affords. When we put the idea of an office out to the team, everyone was game.

The reality was a different story. The travel time and cost in and out of the office was a deal breaker for most of our VAs. Thankfully, we only signed a one-month lease. In the end, we found the experiment to be a costly one and not appropriate for a virtual assistant company. We were still learning and trying new things every day.

For example, we knew that we wanted to write a book about our experience launching the company, so we created a system to document everything. Using an audio recorder app called DropVox, we brain dumped the monthly highlight of activities. The recording was then saved to a Dropbox folder, which triggered a Trello card for our copywriter. He summarized the audio and put the notes in an Evernote notebook, which we then gave to our book editor.

December saw additional changes and improvements to our internal dashboard. Nick added a column called "errors," which showed the team all of the most important tasks. An error could mean a task was past due, the client was the last to respond, or a Trello list had been changed. This change helped to identify the most urgent issues. Also, the dashboard had the capability not only to pull information from Trello but also to push back. VAs were able to update the status of their tasks directly from the dashboard instead of having to go into Trello and drag the card into the dashboard. It sounds like a small improvement, but it was the first step to making the dashboard the central tool.

Because December is a big holiday month, we used the downtime to focus almost exclusively on process and system improvements. We needed to address the client engagement piece as well as some of the internal problems we faced. Slowly, we chipped away at the issues and prepared to start the year off strong in January.

TECH TOOLS

We finally upgraded from the free version of Trello to the business-class version. The business version allowed us to tag boards, which for us were our clients' accounts, and group them into categories, or collections. For example, we could track their status by tagging them, "Former Client," "On Hold," or "Premium." If a client canceled, or a client's credit card failed, we updated the collection so the dashboard only showed the active clients. This saved us from wasting time and money by working on inactive or delinquent clients.

We implemented an internal 5-5-5 Rule, which seemed to be our magic bullet. This rule stated that a VA could have a maximum of five cards in any category at any time, which helped us to focus on task completion. If the VAs were waiting on client feedback to complete a card, the 5-5-5 Rule incentivized them to chase down the client so they could close out the task and pick up another one.

CHAPTER

6

JANUARY

WHAT BUSINESS ARE WE REALLY IN?

Number of client hours delivered: 791
Number of subscribers: 88
Revenue: $29,000

In January, with five good months of operation under our belts, we started to see an increase in customer complaints. In the early months, our tendency was to dismiss unhappy clients as demanding or unrealistic, but it was reaching a level that we could no longer ignore. Ari, in particular, was admittedly defensive and unreceptive to criticism. When we started to lose clients, however, we had to address the problems head on, especially because we relied so heavily on referrals.

Our friend and client, Aaron from Matic Insurance, brought our attention to some issues with the onboarding process. We also received unfavorable feedback from our publisher, Tucker Max at Book In A Box. They both said it wasn't immediately clear how to go about posting a task, and they were bombarded by e-mails. The experience was out of line with the white-glove type of service we promised, and they were annoyed. We were determined to fix the issues and make client onboarding a more streamlined experience.

We started using a systematic process to get to the root cause of a problem called the 5 Whys. First, you state the problem, then you ask, "why," and then you ask "why" four more times until inevitably you arrive at a solution. The method is centered in factual responses and is reliably effective for problem solving on both a small and large scale.

The 5 Whys helped us to examine incidents with clients and improve our service. Anytime something went wrong, it was an opportunity for something to be done better. VAs submitted a form to Ari with a report of the incident and a five-level analysis of why the incident occurred, as well as a proposed solution. The process was directly applicable to the types of problems we were seeing, such as projects coming in late or unhappy clients.

TECH TOOLS

For login management security, we switched from LastPass to 1Password. The benefits were threefold: better user interface, better security, and better customer service. The customer service component was a big one for us. We can't waste time trying to fix or figure things out, so we have to work with companies that offer a stellar customer experience. 1Password met all of our requirements and was simple to implement.

It became clear during this process that some of the VAs were dropping the ball. We'd been cutting them some slack, but our reputation and dependency on referrals were too important to carry any dead weight. We had to let some people go.

BPO: BUSINESS PROCESS OPTIMIZATION

In order to avoid raising money, we had to find clever ways to make money to finance our developments. While we streamlined and improved, we were in talks with some of the most high-profile and successful entrepreneurs in the country, thanks to Joe Polish's Genius Networking event in Arizona. Two months after the event, Ari sent Joe a note to pass along to one of the biggest names in the self-help industry.

Ari said, "Listen, Joe, I'm not sure if it's appropriate, but if you think it is, can you please see to it that Craig Maxwell (due to an NDA, we need to use a pseudonym) gets this note? His presentation at your event really resonated with me, and I want to thank him."

About thirty minutes later, Joe forwarded Ari an audio response from Craig Maxwell himself. It said, "Thank you so much for your message. You don't owe me anything. I'm glad to hear you benefited from the presentation. Joe tells me you're an expert in automating and outsourcing. Maybe there is something my team could learn from your expertise. Here is my personal cell phone."

Just like that, we were directly connected to one of the most influential and powerful businessmen alive today. Ari and Craig Maxwell started texting back and forth. They had two separate calls scheduled, neither of which Craig Maxwell was able to make. Over Christmas, Ari was in Miami with his family when, out of the blue, his phone rang.

It was Craig Maxwell full of apologies. He said, "My schedule has been crazy, I'm so sorry. I'd really like you and your partner to come to my five-day business conference next week. If you guys can stay until Saturday, I'd love you to meet my team and present what you do."

Stunned, Ari called Nick and said, "We're going to Seattle to meet Craig Maxwell and the whole team in person." We were elated.

This was the first time we were talking to a large-scale, extremely high-profile organization about a system we came to call BPO: Business Process Optimization. We were scheduled to fly out to Seattle for our presentation when there was a massive snowstorm in New York. All of the flights out of the tri-state area were grounded, and Ari was stuck. Nick was already in Seattle for the event, so he was able to get to the meeting without incident. We had to Skype Ari into the presentation, which was not ideal, but we did the best we could.

Craig Maxwell, as promised, had his whole team assembled to hear us talk about what we do at Less Doing. There were about twenty-five people in the room. Just like at the Genius Event, we didn't have a formalized presentation or a clear offering for his team at the time. We wanted to demonstrate how we used productivity tools and how those same tools could revolutionize their operation as well. Our main focus was on Trello and Slack. Despite our lack of formality, Craig Maxwell took notes the whole time and loved what we were doing. The presentation lasted close to two hours.

We were invited to put together a proposal to consult with the team and implement a BPO program. We were so excited by the invitation that we had no idea what to charge. We toyed with the idea of doing the work for free and just taking a percentage of the cost savings. They had a pile of inefficiencies that needed cleaning up, but we felt the name association alone would launch us into a new stratosphere.

At the time, we were working with both Joe Polish from Genius and Jay Abraham, the business consulting and strategic marketing expert. We went back and forth with them trying to figure out how to price our services in this new paradigm: high-level consulting. We saw a real opportunity to break into a different market and started to reconsider how we wanted to define ourselves. Jay advised us never to give anything away for free or the clients wouldn't value our offerings. Joe said we should sell a process, not a product. Our good friend and branding expert Claire also pointed out that people don't have what they don't pay for. Those three nuggets were the best advice we ever received, because 1) implementation is a ton of work, 2) it takes a ton of time, and 3) it is a process.

The experience with Craig Maxwell was another turning point for us. We started to realize our real offering was to make businesses more efficient. The VA services were just one way that we could do that. We reexamined and refined what a business efficiency process would look like and recognized the potential was huge.

By design, BPO was completely in line with the Less Doing philosophy of Optimize, Automate, and Outsource. For the optimize piece, we streamlined the way an organization communicates internally through Slack and handles project management with Trello. Phase Two was to automate the majority of an organization's processes, and Phase Three involved leveraging our virtual assistants to outsource all of the tasks that didn't require the unique skills of the employees.

CHAPTER 7

FEBRUARY

—

PARTNERSHIP

Number of client hours delivered: 1,066
Number of subscribers: 80
Revenue: $36,000

THE WORKSHOP

In February, we put most of our time and energy into launching the BPO: Business Productivity Optimization arm of the business. Our meeting with Craig Maxwell in January fueled the idea. Riding the momentum of that meeting, we decided to test BPO's validity by hosting a two-day workshop in New York City. We thought it would be a great way to get proof of concept and gather feedback.

The plan was to see what jived with people and then launch a subscription-based business boot camp. Ari had long hosted personal boot camps through Facebook, and it had been an effective way to engage clients in his coaching services. About twenty people signed up for the two-day workshop.

In typical fashion, we didn't prepare a formal presentation. Our plan was to improvise through interactive demos of various process applications, as we had at Genius in Arizona and with Craig Maxwell's team in Seattle. We had plenty of content to engage people for two days.

We presented well, shared some great information, and answered a lot of questions, but we wound up overwhelming the attendees with a fire hose of information. We both have a tendency to geek out when we talk about our processes. At the end of two days, everyone looked and felt like a deer in headlights, which was not the reaction we were hoping for.

Joe Polish gave us some invaluable feedback at that time. He said people don't pay for value, but they pay for perceived value. He suggested we go around the room and ask everyone for a key take away from the workshop thus far.

Very quickly, we realized this format was not the best use

of our time. Live events are a huge time commitment, and when done correctly, they take a long time to organize. We were still planning to go ahead with the boot camp because we could accommodate an unlimited number of people and present the information in an easier to digest curriculum.

All of the feedback we received after the workshop said we were too technical and provided too much information. In the future, we needed to plan the content and deliver better for the audience.

KAIZEN

We started to reinvest some time and energy back in the company. Based on Toyota's Kaizen system for continual improvement, we started to examine all of our internal processes and systems. Kaizen simply means making "changes for the better." It's not just about productivity; it's about humanizing the workplace and making sure that all of the pieces are functioning in alignment and harmony.

When Toyota, and later Mitsubishi, implemented Kaizen, they had every single member of the company—from the janitors to the executives—submit ideas for improvements. The system was incredibly helpful, not only because of the flow of ideas from the ground up but also because it encouraged a strong culture and sense of community.

People started to see their suggestions implemented, and it fostered an increased desire to improve.

We used a variation of the process and asked all of the VAs to submit an idea a week about how we could make the company better. We weren't looking for ideas that were directly related to their jobs necessarily; we wanted to hear everything. The insight we received was incredibly valuable, and most of the ideas were immediately actionable.

Several suggestions were made about the dashboard, which Nick was able to quickly fix. Some of the VAs asked for clarification about what was considered billable time and what wasn't. This led us to the discovery that the VAs were putting a lot of time into certain activities they didn't know were billable to the clients. We made an adjustment right away so the clients were charged appropriately, and the VAs were accurately compensated for their work.

Meanwhile, Ari's daughter, Chloe, was born in mid-February. Two days after she got home, her temperature dropped dramatically. She had to be monitored in the emergency room for close to a week. Ari and his wife were with her day in and day out, but he was still able to get his work done.

It occurred to us then that there were no excuses for poor

performance. If Ari was able to stay on top of things with everything he had going on, then there was no excuse for anyone else to slack off. No one in the company aside from Nick even knew what was going on with Ari's daughter, because he didn't miss a beat.

We started firing people based on the objective standards we had originally set out, but had been too lenient with. Because our internal system was set up so efficiently, we were able to remove those people within a matter of minutes and without any of our clients' sensitive information being compromised. We were only as good as the perceived value of the VAs.

PARTNERSHIP

In February, we decided to consolidate all of our branding under the Less Doing brand. Up until that point, Ari still had his coaching business, his boot camps, podcasts, and books to promote, and Nick was still working on his app, Calvin. After the workshop, we realized we had one dream and should be one team driving it forward, instead of two people trying to do a million other things under different umbrellas.

This was a huge realization for us and marked another significant turning point for the business. We had always been protective of our friendship, so we put a lot of thought into the matter. The fact that we had complete respect for and trust in one another helped. We never worried that the other person was taking advantage, or was being unfair. If anything, we are overly generous with each other. Ari offered to make Nick a partner in his other LLC for Less Doing, but Nick turned the offer down; he didn't think it made sense. That's the type of partnership that you want to have—one of ultimate trust. We also decided to change the name to Less Doing Virtual Assistants, because no one could pronounce or spell "Less Doists."

Our immediate focus, after rebranding the company Less Doing, was on making the business boot camp a reality. We knew our content and processes were good, but they weren't perfect. Engagement was a challenge because, in our business, we worked almost exclusively with people who had a hard time getting things done. Our clients tended to be unproductive because of the level of overwhelm they tolerated. They didn't answer e-mails; they didn't return calls; they got their schedules mixed up. It was a vicious cycle. Getting them to engage with the process was going to be a hurdle.

DISCOVERY

We were also working on getting the deal with Craig Maxwell solidified. Our objective was to get into the organization, implement some of our processes, and evaluate what worked for them. Going in, we already knew what the problems and the solutions were. They, on the other hand, wanted us to go through a discovery process with each of the individual teams. They felt like we were not listening to them and were trying to steamroll them into solutions that weren't tailored to their needs.

It was an important learning moment: we weren't getting buy-in because people thought we weren't taking their specific needs into account. Because we knew our systems inside and out, we sometimes took it for granted that everyone else was as comfortable with those tools and techniques as we were. This was a similar issue to the one we faced in the workshop.

We faced a lot of hard but critical lessons as we tried to build the business-consulting arm of the company in March. After talking with all of the team members and listening to their needs, our solutions were the same. Three months had passed, and we still had not implemented anything. We thought we had sold them on our plan, but we continued to face pushback.

We were learning the ropes of dealing with a large high-profile company. We felt that 80 percent of the problems with Craig Maxwell's organization could quickly and easily be solved with two applications (Slack and

Trello), but they didn't see it that way. Internal politics at someone else's company are a tough beast to navigate. This experience was a huge part of our learning process as we figured out how we needed to approach different people and organizations.

CHAPTER 8

MARCH

SHIFTING TO BPO

Number of client hours delivered: 980
Number of subscribers: 95
Revenue: $39,000

THE PSYCHOLOGY OF "WORK"

Some people are resistant to automation because they fear it will make their position less significant. They need to feel useful even if their time is not being used wisely. There is a psychological component that goes hand in hand with knowing work is going into a project. People don't like to let go of the illusion of productivity that is created by "work."

The great Harvard social science researcher, Michael Norton, did a whole study on the topic. Sites such as Kayak and Hipmunk have tapped into the psychological satisfaction that accompanies this illusion of "work" with their progress bars. Those bars say, "Please wait while we search and find the best rates for you," and shortly thereafter, lower prices pop up on the screen. When you perceive a greater effort, you feel like you are being taken care of, which makes you want to buy stuff.

Another, less technical example, of this psychological phenomenon is when someone empties the dishwasher. If they do it quietly in the morning, when everyone is still sleeping, they don't get as much credit as they would if they waited until someone hears or sees them doing it.

These behaviors and funny human quirks manifest themselves all the time. Even though we spent thirty minutes on the phone with everyone individually at Craig Maxwell's company, they still felt we weren't able to truly understand their pain points. They remained resistant to our proposed solutions, and we continued to press the same processes we knew to be effective.

There are a few different ways to approach batching and productivity. It comes down to a philosophical question. For example, let's say you had to write one hundred thank you notes. Most people will approach the task systematically, but half of them will write the card, address the envelope, and put a stamp on it, in that order. The other half of them will write all the cards first, then address all of the envelopes, and, finally, stamp each envelope.

The first option is the more psychologically rewarding, but the latter is the most efficient choice. In the first scenario, you can say you're X percent of the way through the task if you are interrupted. The second scenario is the method we applied to Craig Maxwell's organization. We kept getting interrupted because we had to stop and reassess. It looked like nothing was being accomplished, even though progress was being made. There was no cohesion between teams, and no one was communicating with each other.

INTERNAL ADJUSTMENTS

Internally, two of our VAs were training to become BPO specialists. Micala and Florence rose through the ranks quickly and demonstrated a natural aptitude for the high-level business optimization solutions we were proposing to Craig Maxwell & Co. We groomed them on how to do discovery calls, consultations, and implementation. They listened in on our calls and created strategy briefs. They brought their own implementation recommendations to the table, and we saw that they immediately "got it." Micala and Florence took over the production of our weekly webinar and started running the boot camp.

TECH TOOLS

When we launched the BPO boot camp, we offered on-demand video tutorials. We hosted them through Wistia, which is a video hosting site for businesses. It's similar to YouTube but offers a lot more control over who sees what. It also provides analytics and user engagement information. We built a library of video resources for the BPO clients on all the productivity tools and techniques we teach and recommend.

At the end of the month, we set up a billing portal in Chargify, which allowed the clients to access and pay their statements. The response was great because we were nearing tax time and many of the clients had asked for their statements. With the billing portal, they could retrieve them at their convenience and didn't have to wait for someone on our end to get them what they needed. Whenever possible, our goal is to remove bottlenecks, especially internally.

In March, we decided to focus all of our energy and marketing efforts into acquiring more VA clients. Prior to our official partnership, Ari had built a sales funnel to get more people into his personal boot camp. He had just published his second book, *The Art of Less Doing*. With the podcasts and webinars, we had a nice variety of products and services to work with. Once people tapped into our resources, they had a much better understanding of our capabilities and were better equipped to utilize us for increased efficiency.

The VAs were the foundation for all of the rest of our services. Regardless of an individual's or an organization's specific requirements or needs, Less Doing Virtual Assistants became a total business solutions provider. What started as the outsourcing of administrative tasks grew into something far wider reaching and all encompassing, with the VAs at the center of it all.

This critical realization informed the way we positioned ourselves in the market. A friend of Nick's, Hailey, spearheaded a complete overhaul of the Less Doing website to ensure our capabilities were accurately represented. She attended the workshop in exchange for the website redesign (yes, we like to barter). The focus shifted from Ari and his services to the assistants and their range of skills. The site highlighted three core offerings—assistants, consulting, and resources—with an emphasis on business versus personal productivity.

We decided to run Facebook ads to ramp up the volume. Through the ads, we started getting a few new clients a week. Up until that time, there had always been some degree of connection to our clients through referrals or word of mouth. The Facebook clients were completely unknown to us, which was unchartered territory. We started tracking where leads were coming from and which activities led to a spike in interest. The increased number of clients allowed us to stress test our system and continue to make improvements.

With more clients, we raised our prices to $129/month and increased salaries by 10 percent. Nick had been running payroll, but we trained one of the VAs, Casey (who happened to be a CPA), to take over bookkeeping activities, which freed up two hours a week of Nick's time. We switched from weekly to biweekly payments, which then freed up four hours a month of Casey's time. This was an adjustment for the VAs, but a good decision in terms of managing cash flow more efficiently. Delaying payment also allowed us to have more control in case a VA messed up on a task and we wanted to adjust the billable time.

We started to use Amazon's free coworking, pop-up space. We used it to meet with each other on a regular basis, but the team continued to work from home, or the library, or wherever they felt they could get the most work done. Environment is directly related to productivity, and we didn't believe that being together physically was necessary to foster a team culture. Our team loved their work and they loved the freedom, so the culture followed suit.

APRIL

A REAL BUSINESS

Number of client hours delivered: 1,211
Number of subscribers: 100
Revenue: $30,000

STREAMLINING THE SYSTEMS

In April, because of the influx of clients and the shift in our services to BPO, we implemented a "three strikes and you're out" employment policy. This allowed us to swiftly get rid of VAs who were not pulling their weight or dropping the ball. Overall, the system worked well for us because it was objective. People knew where they stood and why.

Admittedly, strikes were a little subjective, but it came down to common sense. If a VA told a client he or she would get on the person's project immediately but then didn't update anyone for three days, the VA would get a strike. Or, if there was an issue with a client but the VA didn't notify anyone about it, a strike was issued. Also, VAs were permitted to work any hours they wanted, but if they were going away for a few days and didn't notify anyone or off-loaded their tasks, we had a problem. If someone won the weekly bonus, his or her strike was subtracted.

Also in April, Ari implemented quarterly reviews for all of the VAs. At Less Doing, these reviews were ten-minute, one-on-one conversations to discuss quarterly goals and progress. We borrowed Google's OKR[4] (Objective Key Results) practice and made it our own. One of our VAs created the metrics and the questions that focused on what would be accomplished within the next ninety days.

- What is your time commitment?
- How do you believe we can best deliver high-quality service to our clients?
- How will you specifically contribute?
- In what areas would you like to personally improve?

---

4   https://library.gv.com/how-google-sets-goals-okrs-a1f69b0b72c7#.ooset2rcz

The VA responses were captured in Evernote. At the end of ninety days, they were revisited, progress was assessed, and promotions were determined accordingly.

At that point, we had about fourteen VAs and considerably more specialists. Our stance has always been that if someone asks us to do something, we'll do it. We never said no to a project (as long as it was legal). The only time a client made a request that we had to decline was when we were asked to complete a fourteen-hour continuing education course for a real estate license and then certify that the client had completed it. Even if we didn't have the skill set in-house to complete an assignment, we had the resources to find the right people. Whenever we found someone who did a great job, without hesitation, we tried to get that person to join the team.

Joining the team entailed joining our Slack, Trello, and the internal dashboard, as well as filling out some electronic paperwork. It could not have been simpler. We had specialists to handle travel, audio and video production, sales, social media, infographics, marketing, legal, project management, and more. As the business evolved, we implemented more and more structure to the company. We started having weekly meetings for finances, BPO, and strategy. By hiring an accountant and a lawyer, and introducing quarterly reviews, we started to look and operate more like a legitimate company.

On the client side, we made a few changes to make it more difficult for them to cancel if they were unhappy with the service. We wanted to build in opportunities to save the relationship whenever possible. When we started using the Chargify self-service page, there was an option to cancel. We had that option removed so the client needed to e-mail us instead.

We started to be better organized and aware of how money flowed in and out of the company. There was an event called Mastermind Talks coming up in May, which was an invitation-only event for entrepreneurs. Ari had previously been invited, and this was Nick's first opportunity to go. The ticket to get there was $7,000. Nick wasn't able to attend due to the cost and a scheduling conflict, but it raised the issue of how could we fairly use company money for expenses without one person benefiting more than the other.

We resolved the matter by setting up two additional checking accounts that were linked to the master account. On a monthly basis, we transferred the same amount of money from the master account to the two subaccounts to cover individually incurred business expenses. It was a clever, fair, and totally transparent way to keep track of what we were spending.

TECH TOOLS

One of our clients, Steve, told us he wanted a better system to see how many hours remained on his plan. The onus of doing the calculation fell to the client, and we never wanted to ask the client to do any work. At first, Casey manually updated a Trello card with the time remaining, which took an hour of her time every week and was subject to human error. Later, Brit (our CTO, chief technology officer) built a custom integration between Trello and Toggl. The Trello card was automatically updated every day with the client's remaining hours. The information was sent to the client in a weekly e-mail. This is a great example of how we followed the Less Doing OAO process by optimizing and then automating. Although there was some manual work on our end, at least we had taken it off the client's plate.

We started to expand our services even further in April. Some of our clients expressed interest in custom dashboards for their project management needs. They had seen the one Nick created for Less Doing at the workshop and wanted something similar for their own companies.

Only businesses that were really in the swing with optimization and automation benefited from a customized dashboard. Those that were doing really well with their processes understood the dashboard could give them the optics necessary to run a company. Most of our clients were already using Trello. Their application programming interface (API) allowed us to customize the information we wanted to pull, and then we could format the information in a way that made the most sense for their particular goals. At that point, we had more experience building customized dashboards than any other provider in our space.

OUTSOURCING INTERNALLY

Ari is a master of operations; he has a firm handle on his schedule, his capabilities, his workload, and his ability to optimize, automate, and outsource. It makes sense; he developed the process. He was working closely with a woman named Alana, who became his semi-dedicated VA. She took care of everything he needed to off-load and absorbed the "Dashboard Police" role, which freed up about thirty minutes of Ari's evenings. This meant going through the dashboard and taking note of anyone who was late on a card or who hadn't responded to a card in a few days. Then Alana contacted the VA responsible for the project to see what was going on and how the card could be moved forward.

For two weeks, she went through the process very thoroughly and was able to intercept a handful of potential issues. She did such a good job with it, Ari asked her to become the general manager. This was a huge step, because up until then, he'd been managing the dashboard and the team himself, which was very time consuming.

Nick started to off-load the majority of his tasks to another one of our top VAs, Casey. Even if she didn't know how to do something, Nick invested the time to get her up to speed, knowing that in the end, it would save him time. She took over payroll, client payment problems, and some of the other financial reporting.

Within the month, we had off-loaded our two biggest time sinks internally. We took a huge step away from operations to focus on long-term solutions and strategies, always with scalability in mind. On both the VA and BPO sides of the business, we knew it didn't make long-term sense for us to be the ones completing tasks or consulting with clients. We had to get the VAs ready to absorb some of the day-to-day responsibilities. Off-loading to Alana and Casey was a big leap forward.

The framework for Less Doing is Optimize, Automate, and Outsource, in that order. Many people would consider what we did with Alana and Casey outsourcing. We've even referred to it that way ourselves. The truth is, what we did with them was optimize their skill set. Casey was better suited to handle financial tasks than Nick. Therefore, she did it better and in less time.

We strive for people to focus on their unique abilities. We did this with our clients by helping them off-load tasks they shouldn't be doing, and we did it internally too. We helped people understand the OAO framework and how to use it to allocate resources such as time, money, or people properly. One of Ari's unique abilities is creating content. He's a human encyclopedia when it comes to tools and productivity services. Nick's unique ability is taking complex systems or processes and creating elegant and simple technical solutions. We constantly tried to free up as much time for each other as possible so we could each focus on our competitive advantages.

Because our clients looked to us for optimization solutions, we had to be constantly on top of new apps and updates. We wanted to be able to recommend other businesses with the utmost confidence and assurance. Sometimes upgrades and system changes were subtle, or we bullishly stuck with certain services that had been eclipsed.

TECH TOOLS

We started using a tool called Front, which is a team-aggregated inbox that allowed us to connect multiple communication sources such as texts, e-mails, Facebook, or Twitter. Using this tool, anyone on the team who managed the company e-mail was able to provide incoming inquiries with a faster response. Instead of forwarding messages, we simply assigned the message to a specific person.

We also set up Twilio, which is a cloud-based communications service to manage phone calls and text messages, and connected it to Front. The idea was to allow our clients the capability to text us urgent tasks.

We were always trying to remove bottlenecks. The shared phone number allowed us to get rid of a big one. Certain websites (such as Stripe) required a two-step authentication process to login. We typed in the password, and they texted a verification code, which was only valid for a brief, fixed window of time. If Casey wanted to login to our Stripe account, she had to text Nick to get the code. Not only did this create a bottleneck, but many times Nick didn't see her text within the allotted time frame, and they had to start the login process all over again. By switching to the team phone number, the bottleneck was removed; we saved Casey an annoying step, and she was able to complete the task faster.

One final tech implementation was Smooch, which is a chat feature used on the website. Smooch allowed us to chat directly with people while they were browsing our website and answer their questions. Tools such as Smooch were a huge source of lead generation for us. There were often questions from interested clients about what we were capable of doing. Many times, the difference between a sale and a lost lead was a single timely answer. Anytime a new user popped up with a question on Smooch, we got an adrenaline rush to see who got to it faster and ultimately won a new client.

For example, Ari had long been a big fan of Schedule Once, a calendar management tool. Scheduling is a huge piece in the productivity puzzle, so the right system can make or break efficiency. Admittedly, Ari had the tendency to stick with certain apps over others if he was happy with the job they performed. Unless something was remarkably better, he usually wouldn't even consider it. This is what happened with Calendly.

For years, people had been extolling its features and ease, but he preferred Schedule Once. The noise around Calendly increased, and Nick insisted he give it another look. Because Nick had developed his own scheduling tool with Calvin, he was very familiar with the space. He was right; the app had been vastly improved, and it now included the functionality Ari had been looking for. The program can be used by individuals or by a team. You can identify priorities, appoint a team leader, and optimize the best time slot available for everyone. It also handles collective booking, which we used with our podcasts.

Ari made an announcement in the company newsletter about the significant changes and officially gave Calendly his recommendation. Nick was quick to point out that because of the position we were in as thought leaders and productivity experts, we needed to be well versed in what was out there, even if we weren't using the tools ourselves. We could not blindly recommend Salesforce over another CRM software if we hadn't revisited all of the options on a regular basis. Being knowledgeable and assessing the marketplace gave us an edge, as we were constantly looking for best practices.

The technology tools allowed us to optimize our own OAO framework. Not many start-up owners delegate to the degree we were able to within the first year of business. In fact, we can't think of anyone who scaled and off-loaded to the degree we did, but being first isn't what drove us. It was a win-win for everyone. We were able to focus on things that we were uniquely qualified to do, and the VAs were as well. We were growing up and growing into our own philosophy.

CHAPTER

10

MAY

___

VISION

Number of client hours delivered: 1,489
Number of subscribers: 112
Revenue: $46,000

WHITE LABEL

Still three months shy of our one-year birthday, our attention shifted to the future. It appeared to be bright, but we wanted to be strategic about own growth plan.

Several of our clients inquired about the possibility of white labeling our services. Specifically, one of our clients, Dean, wanted to introduce new techniques to apply to the real estate market. We met him through Joe, and our services resonated with him immediately. He wanted to investigate the potential behind a concept called "Less Doing for Real Estate Marketing."

Our friend Steve was working on a concept that was a high-end version of FoundersCard. He wanted us to provide the customer service and fulfillment. Our other friend, Aaron, wanted to build a product that would help make meetings more efficient. More frequently, people started to approach us for these types of affiliate partnerships, where we would facilitate the back end of their businesses.

Nick was invited to speak at a prestigious salon with a collection of other interesting industry influencers. It was there that Nick met the founder of the number-one online lifestyle guide for the modern man. He was interested in what we were doing with Less Doing. We set up a meeting to discuss how he could help us develop some business partnerships and be a general advisor.

Even before we started receiving inquiries, Nick envisioned that we would leverage all of our resources (VAs and our marketing specialists) and roll out an incubator where we built exclusively internal projects for other companies. The first projects under the Less Doing incubator would be Calvin and Less Doing Peak Time, a tool to help people identify their most productive hours of the day. Eventually, the internal dashboard would be a consumer-facing project management software with the best elements of Trello, Asana, and Virtual Assistants built directly into the platform.

With our ace team in place, we were well positioned to offer end-to-end solutions for other companies too. We wanted to be more involved in helping other business owners and entrepreneurs build their companies. Our team of VAs and specialists knew how to solve virtually any problem, or figure out the best solution. In turn, we'd only build and strengthen our own products and services. We started to explore some of these relationships and opportunities in May.

CLIENT ENGAGEMENT

Nir Eyal, the well-known behavioral psychologist, had some fantastic ideas for us about the client onboarding process. We had made some improvements since the onboarding complaints rose to the surface back in January, but there was always room for improvement.

At the time, someone from our team spent about fifteen minutes on the phone with a new client. We used that time to show them the mechanics of our service. We showed them how to use Trello, how to post and track a task, and made sure that by the end of the call, at least one task was inputted.

Nir knew that our problem was never customer acquisition; it was customer engagement. We struggled to find a way to get people to truly buy in to the services we recommended. He suggested that we spend at least an hour on the phone with new clients in order to learn everything we could about them, especially what was going wrong for them, both professionally and personally.

This was a brilliant insight coming from the expert on "sticky" services. He acknowledged that our product ticked all of the boxes for a perfect sticky product. The customer lifetime value was super high because people stayed with us. It was well worth the investment to spend as much time as necessary to get the customers up and running. Once we showed them our value and started learning their specific preferences, we had them hooked on the service.

Most people have no idea how much they can off-load. There are so many things they think only they can do, but it's just not the case, especially these days. We needed to spend more time with people upfront—as much time as possible. Nir had a good point. His argument was that if we could really understand where people were coming from, we could offer them even better solutions. They'd be so committed to the process and the services after they saw the potential, they would never leave.

Based on Nir's suggestion, we immediately switched to longer onboarding phone calls. The change was swift and significant. We off-loaded the calls to our best VAs in the trenches, who had a firm handle on customizing business solutions.

This process worked beautifully because the VAs were able to say, "Hey, I know you need X, Y, and Z accomplished immediately, but you seem like a really good candidate for private coaching." Or, "Your business sounds complex. Are you interested in learning more about some of our BPO resources?" The onboarding process became an amazing sales opportunity for our most knowledgeable and skilled VAs to offer the full spectrum of our products and services to new clients.

THE SALES FUNNEL

Thanks to Nir's advice, we had a system to keep people fully engaged when they signed up. Once we figured out we would primarily drive our clients toward signing up for VA services, which took us a few months, it was time to beef up our lead acquisition efforts.

There are many different ways to drives sales. We decided

to use the video from the Genius Event in October '15, which was three-and-half-hours long. After some investigating, we chose to roll out something called a "self-liquid offer." This means that the main offer should offset the cost of Facebook ads, or whatever marketing costs are incurred. From the main offer, you then try to upsell or down sell additional products. In theory, the funnel is supposed to cover itself, and any sales that come out of it are gravy.

The main offer of the Genius video started at $47. The upsell was the VA monthly services at $129 a month, and the down sell was a video course about e-mail efficiency and virtual systems. Everything was geared to get people primed for the VA services.

We hired a world-class copywriter named Sue to compose the e-mails. We'd never used an e-mail copywriter at that level before, but it seemed worth it at $275 per e-mail. She created an SOS sequence, or soap opera sequence, which is a technical way of saying she told a story that would lead into a sales offer. Andre Chaperon, who, coincidentally, was a big fan of Ari's first book and introduced us to Sue, created the concept.

We started building the funnel through ClickFunnels. We linked the Facebook ads and immediately started getting some traction. We ran AB testing, which compares two websites to see which one performs better, so we could determine which pages were getting the most conversions. About two weeks in, we changed the offer.

We started charging $97 for the main offer video. We figured it would be easier for people to make the jump to $129/month for VA services from there than from $47. If they said no to the VA package, we offered a $47/month membership to our Less Doing Boot Camp, which is an online coaching program.

Regardless of whether they signed up or not, once someone was in the funnel, they started to receive the SOS e-mails. All of the communication and the products were designed to drive people back to the VA services, and it was a very effective strategy. We're still using the same funnel today.

HIGH-PROFILE IMPLEMENTATION

Meanwhile, we were still working on the engagement with Craig Maxwell and his team. They wanted us to get training in their project management philosophy and integrate it with Slack and Trello. We were still determined to figure out a way to work with them.

Once we learned their project management system, we

realized it was in line with how we approached PM with other organizations. There were a few key differences, but overall, the workflow component was familiar. Unlike our system, theirs required a single owner. We learned that if more than one person owns something in a large organization, effectively, no one owns it. Accountability goes out the window. Once we figured out a way to integrate their system with Trello, Craig's team could work the way they were accustomed to working while also utilizing a highly effective new tool.

Out of the blue, Craig Maxwell's executive assistant resigned. He was making some internal staffing changes and saw an opportunity to revisit our services with fresh eyes. Craig reached out directly and invited us to work with him and his team on getting our systems incorporated. This was our chance to get in front of everyone one more time and drive home the value of our offering.

Within four days, Nick built a custom dashboard to demonstrate how the integrated systems could work for the entire organization. We were slotted for a two-hour meeting, but Nick knew from previous experience not to schedule his flight home until the next day. We were there with John's team for seven straight hours. Nick talked so much that he lost his voice.

Craig said the dashboard was "brilliant," and the executive team was ready to move forward with implementation. Nick got the team set up on Slack and showed them how to use it. This team was ingrained with texting and e-mailing, even though they were exhausted by it. By the end of the day, they had fallen in love with Slack. They experienced the communication efficiency as soon as Nick walked them through a demo.

Right away, Slack reduced their e-mail volume by 50 percent. It also made it easier to schedule time with them since they were all using the same system. Their questions were answered immediately and efficiently and there were no bottlenecks. They absolutely loved it, and the meeting was a huge victory for them and us. Finally, this team was starting to hum as efficiently as we knew they could all along.

The meeting was illuminating in several ways. From a strategic point of view, we realized where we had gone wrong with the company for the last few months and why they were slow to buy in. We should have insisted that Phase One be Slack implementation for everyone and Phase Two be Trello, instead of trying to implement both at the same time in smaller groups. Slack is considerably easier to implement than Trello, and it creates a much larger initial impact. People are able to see the benefits immediately, but everyone has to use it for it to be effective. Also, it's much easier to set Trello up if you can communicate in Slack.

We also realized that we needed to start at the top of the organization and work our way down. Craig had always been excited about our processes, but we lost him somewhere along the line to the other decision makers within the organization. Because Craig was committed and we had top-level executive buy-in, the rest of the teams followed suit.

Another huge plus for us this time around was that we were able to work with a single internal liaison to help with implementation. At a huge corporation, you need to have both the head boss and someone else on the inside to drive the plan forward. Our liaison was instrumental in ironing out the kinks and helping us get set up. If and when we work with another large organization, we'll know to start with the lead decision maker and ask for one internal person to be nominated to help us implement the changes. We'll also start with Slack to get widespread, immediate buy-in for effective team communication.

CONTINUED INTERNAL IMPROVEMENTS

Back at home, we made a company decision to simplify how people purchased from us. Up until May, we allowed clients to determine the number of service hours they wanted through Chargify. The default number was ten. This meant that when people went to the checkout, the default shopping cart was $529 (or, $129 + $40/hr * 10 hr). This was a big number, especially considering they didn't yet understand the value of the service. Eventually, Ari had a great idea to simply by offering one option on the site, which was to sign up for the $129 and get five hours for free. Based on Nir's input, we rationalized that people would be hooked on the service after the five free hours.

In order to customize the experience, we needed to hire a developer who could customize automations between our various tools. Specifically, we needed to trigger a client's account to default to a certain number of hours when they signed up in Chargify.

Chargify provided us with a list of their consultants and on it, Nick found Brit out of San Francisco. Brit used to be the head of Chargify's sales department, so we were beyond lucky to find him on a list of random names. Initially, we only used him for internal projects, but he's helped us tremendously. He figured out the website and Chargify integration as well as the Toggl API.

Hiring Brit marked a significant move toward further automation. He was an expert in that area and found countless numbers of ways to reduce steps and simplify processes. He had extensive experience building off of Zapier's platform as well as vast knowledge about some of the key tools we used, such as Intercom, Stripe, segment.io, and of course Chargify. Although automation has always been top of mind for us, Brit introduced customized automation solutions that took us to an entirely new level.

Brit and Nick started to focus on the dashboard and its seemingly infinite potential. Nick saw it as the heart of the business, and he laid out a roadmap of his vision. At that point, there was one company login, so everyone saw the same screen. Nick wanted to give all of the VAs their own login so they could set up their availability. If VAs were working on something, they appeared in red as "busy"; likewise, if they were free, they appeared in green. If they were nearing the end of a project, they appeared in yellow. That way, any of the managers could scan the dashboard and immediately see who was red, yellow, or green and optimize who should work on specific tasks up next in the queue.

We also wanted to clean up the design and the overall functionality. At that point, the dashboard was simply used as a viewing tool to see what needed to be done. The VAs selected projects but had to move the cards into Trello and make notes there. Nick's eventual goal was for the VAs to be able to do and see everything in the dashboard without even using Trello to simplify task management further. He also had a vision of developing a tool that could be used for any of the businesses we worked with, not just our own.

Eventually, the dashboard would be able to tell the VAs exactly what they should be working on at any given time. All functionality had this goal in mind. Key features included a priority section, snooze capability, and internal notes, not just to save time to scan, but to make sure that important things weren't missed.

To achieve the desired level of functionality, the dashboard needed to be streamlined further and cleaned up. Nick wanted only the most relevant information so VAs could quickly know what they need to do, whether it was picking up a task or responding to a client.

The ultimate goal is for the clients to stop using Trello too. His vision is to create one Less Doing platform where clients can see everything they need to see, post tasks, and manage their accounts all at the same time and from the same place. We will integrate with tools such as Asana and Trello to make it very easy for people to post tasks to our dashboard from their current accounts. It will eventually be a free project management software for consumers, and if they want to use the VAs, they can pay for the services. Imagine having a to-do list where you can click a button and have someone else do it!

Strategically, Nick decided to start with the VA dashboard because improving the client experience and making sure we are doing tasks efficiently and effectively was the highest priority. Also, since the VAs were using the dashboard daily to do their jobs more effectively, Nick had a valuable, built-in resource for feedback about what was working, what wasn't, and what needed improvement. He had close to thirty VAs using the board at any given time, all trained in efficiency and productivity. What better test market could he ask for?

May marked a big turning point in terms of thinking ahead strategically. Up until then, we faced the problems that were immediately in front of us and worked quickly to figure out solutions. For the first time, we took a step back to look at the big picture of where we were going.

CHAPTER

11

JUNE

METRICS

Number of client hours delivered: 1,526
(647 Internal / 879 External)
Number of subscribers: 136
Revenue: $50,000

THE DATA WILL SET YOU FREE

Our focus shifted from systems to metrics. Nick, with over eight years on Wall Street as a high-frequency algorithmic trader and with a master's in financial engineering from Berkeley, embraced the numbers. We paid attention to a few key measurements. The first was our customer churn rate, which is the percentage of clients who cancel our services within a given time frame. It's basically the drop-off rate. Our goal was for churn to be as low as possible. At the time, it was around 11 percent, which is not a bad start.

TECH TOOLS

We set up a tool called ChartMogul, which told us the customer Lifetime Value (LTV) of each client, as well as our growth and churn rates. With a little bit of development work, we were able to track each client to his or her source and evaluate churn rates in relation to the number of hours of service. For example, what was the churn rate if a client spent twenty hours with us versus five? Or, what was the churn rate and lifetime value of a customer we got from a Facebook ad versus from Genius Network versus our podcast? Facebook had a famous data scientist, Chamath Palihapitiya, who figured out if someone adds seven friends in the first ten days of signing up, that person is 90 percent more likely to be an active customer. In our case, our hunch was if someone used ten hours or more, that person would stick around.

Nick also set up segment.io, where all of the data for analytics is aggregated. It connected to the various data sources and was linked to a Postgres database. All of our e-mail, Facebook ads, hours logged, revenue, and any other relevant metrics were fed to one central location. With all of the information in one place, we started running interesting analytics through Mode.

Mode is a business intelligence tool that allows you to custom code metrics and whatever analysis you want. Using Mode, Nick created an analytics dashboard, which showed all of the inactive clients that Ari should get in touch with. This was the best leading indicator of churn we could find.

We found that nearly 80 percent of our clients used the service on a weekly basis. We preferred to have a core base of clients who logged hundreds of hours a month than hundreds of clients who only logged a few hours here and there. Ideally, we didn't want anyone to be inactive for more than a two-week stretch. Mode helped us to identify the outliers so we could proactively reach out and get them engaged again. Because of our mantra—Optimize, Automate, Outsource—our clients assumed we outsourced everything. Because of that assumption, when one of us made a call or sent a direct e-mail, it had a pretty significant impact.

Further examples of things we used Mode for were seeing the total number of hours we owed to our clients, calculating payroll, viewing the average number of months a client stayed, the LTV of a client conditional on how they became a client (podcast, Facebook ads, book, etc.). This gave us actionable data, which drove our business decisions. For instance, our LTV might be $1,000 on average, but only $100 for people came from Facebook ads. This information let us know exactly how much we should budget on Facebook.

The second key metric we started actively tracking was the amount of internal work the VAs were logging versus external. In May, we hovered around 25 percent. We knew that this would increase after hiring Brit, but it would be an investment that would pay off in the long run. He would help us to automate various tasks that we had been doing manually. We were actively working on growing the business by creating our technology, building the sales funnel, editing the podcast, dashboard policing, payroll, and an assortment of other growth-centric tasks.

We were a completely different service four months previously than we were in May, and some of the clients weren't aware of the vast changes and improvements that had been made. One of our clients, Nico, was traveling for a month. When he got home and logged onto Less Doing, he e-mailed Ari immediately and said, "This is like a completely different company. It was good before, but now it's amazing." That's the kind of feedback we live for. Also, Trello reached out to us, because, apparently, we were one of their top-five users (out of 16 million). For a company that wasn't even a year old, we considered this to be a huge achievement and a pretty cool way to get noticed.

We found a new way of working together, in which Nick figured out what we should focus on with a data-driven approach, and Ari figured out a way to execute (Nick is the traffic controller and Ari is the pilot). In any business, it's just as important to know what to work on as it is to know *how* you're going to do it. Doing low-priority tasks efficiently doesn't move the needle.

AUTOMATION AT HOME

We were invited to do a presentation for one of New York's premier, high-caliber executive assistant placement firms.[5] We decided to share the same information that we had at Joe's Genius Network Event. Only this time, we were better prepared. One of our VAs put together a comprehensive video.[6] Our three-and-half-hour presentation had been refined to an hour and a half. Our pitch was twice as efficient as it had been just six months before and was even better received.

Our presentation was for a group of high-level executive assistants, all of whom were making well over $100,000 a year. We went into the event thinking we would attract a few new clients, but we wound up hearing from a handful of people who wanted to become VAs. This happened almost every time we were in front of a group of people. They thought the work sounded fun and interesting, and they wanted to be a part of it. For them, it was more about the learning opportunity than the money.

---

5   https://lessdoists.wistia.com/medias/swlzgejoyz
6   https://lessdoists.wistia.com/medias/11ubh62jtp

Despite the continued incredible response to the company, we still made a few rookie mistakes. In June, we decided to pay ourselves for the first time, but we were premature in that decision. We underestimated how much we needed to reinvest into the company for technology. We struggled to find a system that would help us to monitor our costs better. You'd think a guy from the finance world and a productivity architect would have had this piece nailed down, but we didn't at all.

We didn't have a system to track how much we spent on our various development projects and there was no follow-up. One time, we found ourselves in the hairy situation of realizing payroll was due in four days, but we were $20,000 in the hole. We hadn't looked at the credit card charges in a while, and they had stacked up quickly.

We'd been so focused on the metrics and the analytics that we weren't paying enough attention to the projects or hours in Toggl. This was something we both needed to manage more efficiently, which was our initial solution to the problem. Nick's vision was to have everything—financials, payroll, churn, number of clients, number of active projects, priorities, VA availability—plugged into the internal dashboard. Until Nick built the dashboard of his dreams, we patched things together with our existing tools.

We used a tool called Sway in Slack that told us how much money we had in the bank and how much we owed on the credit card. Sway didn't tell us how much the upcoming payroll would be, however, since that information was located in Toggl. It was fed into our database, and we are able to calculate it and print it on our analytics dashboard.

In June, we became increasingly aware of our liability. We had been selling credits to clients or giving them away for free if there was an issue. For example, we had one thousand unused hours of client credit stored up, which equaled roughly $30,000. If all of those clients wanted to use their hours at the same time, we would be screwed. It was a highly unlikely scenario, but still, we were vulnerable.

We logged the free client hours in Toggl, but there was no way to trace them or keep a record of those promised hours. If we ever wanted to figure out where a client was in terms of hours, or if, god forbid, Toggl went down, there was no way to validate how many hours the clients were owed.

Our new developer, Brit, suggested we switch our policy from handing out hours when there were issues, which were impossible to track, to giving monetary credit. If someone was upset, we credited his or her account $100.

When their monthly subscription rate of $129 was owed, they were only charged $29. It was a subtle change, but a much cleaner way to keep track of what we owed.

Our process of charging clients was to sit down every Monday and go through all of the outstanding projects. Nick and Casey saw who had used their credit; Casey automatically charged them for additional hours, and then she updated the information to Toggl. On average this process took about an hour and a half. More importantly, though, there was a high risk for error. Turns out, people get pretty pissed off when they are accidentally charged.

We believed an investment in automation would pay off in the long term. An hour here, ten or twenty minutes there, add up quickly, and we wanted Casey, and all of our VAs to work primarily on tasks that really interested them, instead of chasing their tails doing menial paperwork.

We started to look for additional ways to tighten the reigns and better assess where we were spending money. For internal work, the VAs tagged their Trello cards within one of eight different categories. This way, we could better assess how they spent their time, whether it was on onboarding calls, accounting, or development projects. If there was a big cost, we were able to spot it quickly.

TECH TOOLS

June was an aggressive month for setting up automations and streamlining activities. We switched from MailChimp to ActiveCampaign to send out our weekly e-mail newsletters. ActiveCampaign was integrated with our website, so we had much better information on the paths our clients took to get to us. We could pinpoint their arrival and track their behavior. For example, if a new client came in through a specific podcast, we could see that he or she signed up for our newsletter, didn't open the first three automated e-mails, opened the fourth, and clicked on the offer. This quality of data was critical to making marketing decisions and assessing which initiatives were effective.

We also switched from Smooch to Intercom for live chats on the website. Intercom was a better solution for us to get in front of people. If someone visited the pricing page three times, we could pop in to see if the person had a question. If someone's browser was in German, we could pipe up and let that person know that we had German-speaking VAs. It also serves as a shared inbox, so any one of us could respond to a client or lead request, which brought our response time way down. We sent custom weekly e-mails to clients to tell them how much time we saved them, what tasks we completed, and what tasks we were waiting for them to respond to.

> We were able to make all of these improvements because of the custom integrations we set up. Using segment.io made it easy to feed all of our data from Trello, Toggl, and Chargify into a central database. We were then able to build scripts to automate tasks using information from across services. For example, e-mails to clients were automatically generated regarding how many hours we saved them (from Toggl) and how many tasks we completed (from Trello).

Because of the improved systems, we started to take some time away from the business. Nick went to Israel for two weeks and the business wasn't impacted at all. Ari and his family routinely go to the Hamptons for the entire summer, and that year was no different.

Ari could send a quick note to Nick while he got his kids in the car, rather than waiting until we had time to talk. One of the key tools that made this possible was an app called Roger. It's basically a walkie-talkie that allowed us to send near real-time voice messages to each other. We rarely had phone calls because asynchronous communication allowed us to send messages at a time that worked for us; the other could listen at a time that worked for him and then respond in kind. One of the many benefits was 1.5 times playback speed. Roger also allowed us to have multiperson conversations. The company was set up in a way that we were able to enjoy all the perks of working remotely, just like our VAs. We were still able to participate in the day-to-day and meet our commitments.

STILL LEARNING

One of our clients approached us in May about developing an app. Ari and the client went back and forth negotiating the project, but the scope had not been defined. No one really even knew what was being negotiated. We learned that Nick needed to always be involved in conversations that concerned big tech projects.

It was a huge learning moment for us because we were still weighing the types of projects we should be involved with. There are a lot of pros to app development, but our time was extremely limited. In this client's case, he wanted to possibly integrate our VAs for support, and it would have been an opportunity to build a recurring revenue source. Even though we said yes to every project, we were growing up and needed to start focusing. We decided to shelve it for the time being because it was too much of a distraction from our focus of growing the company.

Throughout June, we talked a lot about how much we charged our clients. We needed a cash infusion into the business and raising the prices seemed to be a natural way of doing that. We went back and forth on the discussion multiple times. We were at $40/hr and $129/month. Mid-month, we raised our prices to

$50/hr and $149/month. In two weeks, no one new signed up.

We asked ourselves the following questions: Did we raise the rate too much? Should we drop the rates back down again quickly before anyone notices? The bigger questions, however, were as follows: What should our strategy be for rate increases? When should we do it and by how much? Was there some sort of trigger we should have had in place? What information would that trigger be reliant upon? A low churn rate was a good indicator, and we both agreed client retention was a high priority, but signing new clients was important too. As we closed out our eleventh month in business, we faced some critical financial and operational issues, all of which needed to be addressed immediately if we were going to scale.

We decided to roll back to the original pricing. Any change of this sort needed to be backed by data. If we wanted to raise the price, we had to A/B test it, quantify the effect of a price increase, and know exactly how many more (or fewer) people signed up as a result of the increase. One way to measure pricing changes was to run two different Facebook ads at different pricing pages, but we decided to stop running Facebook ads until our churn was below 5 percent (it was at 11 percent). Our two biggest takeaways were 1) there's no sense in investing in scalability prematurely, and 2) if you can't measure it, don't change it.

CHAPTER

12

JULY

REAL-LIFE ISSUES

Number of client hours delivered: 1,393
(478 Internal / 915 External)
Number of subscribers: 144
Revenue: $103,000

July marked our one-year birthday. We crossed out of the "start-up" phase and dealt with real-world issues that grown-up companies face. With thirty VAs and one hundred specialists, our team had grown to accommodate the influx of subscribers and projects. There were some setbacks balanced out by significant improvements.

Of particular note, our engagement with Craig Maxwell and his company came to an end. We had already completed two out of the three phases of the contract: discovery and implementation. They decided they wanted to take over the third phase of the agreement on their own.

Ever the optimist, Ari saw the relationship as a success even though the company canceled its contract. He rationalized that it had been an amazing experience working with such a high-profile organization; we learned valuable communication and presentation strategies, and we were better off because of it. Nick, on the other hand, took the news badly because he hoped Craig Maxwell's company would want to continue the relationship into phases four, five, and six. He agreed we had learned some valuable lessons though.

Even though we have the same personality type, and are similar in most ways, we see the glass from very different angles. It's been a positive balance because you can't have a high-functioning, high-growth company with two optimists or two pessimists at the helm.

The big takeaway from the experience with Craig Maxwell was that we didn't structure the deal for success. It was a perpetual consulting agreement. On top of that, we were dealing with extraordinarily busy people. They barely had five minutes to spare, let alone the time to invest in learning new systems they didn't understand the value of. We decided in the future, if a large company wanted to engage us, we'd approach the arrangement differently. If we simply fly out and charge a day rate, we can implement everything in person within a few days and get buy-in across the board.

ANALYTICS AND COST SAVINGS

We moved away from subjective decision making and focused more intensely on quantitative metrics. In June, we had started looking at churn rates and implemented some rules regarding earned revenue and expenditures. For example, we decided not to pay ourselves unless we were bringing in at least $20,000 a month of recurring revenue.

We were considerably more intentional about every aspect of the business. We wanted to have a better understanding of how and where the money flowed and how we could improve our cash flow. Compared to other founders, we still had a relaxed approach, but we wanted to be more organized and conscientious.

We'd been running the business at a loss for several months because we were reinvesting more than the earnings back into the company. Things were a little tense at times around this discussion. Ari is financially conserva-tive, because he's been burned in business before, and the experience left him cautious. On the other hand, Nick tends to be more aggressive with taking risk (perhaps this is the trader in him). He knew the internal improvements would be well worth the investment. In the trading world he came from, people used to say, "Sometimes, you just have to put your balls on the table." He advocated a similar strategy in July. Because of Nick's confidence, and Ari's confidence in Nick, we were able to work through it and push forward.

HUSTLE AND FLOW

How a company grows is a choice. We could either grow slowly and curb costs, or we could make larger invest-ments, take on a little bit of debt, hustle our butts off, and grow very quickly. We didn't want to curb the investment we were making for internal improvements, because everything we had cooking was critical to our future success. We chose the hustle path and looked for ways to 1) save cash, 2) get more clients, and 3) improve qual-ity control.

We threw ourselves in the deep end and backed ourselves against a wall, but we knew it would pay off. Everything we worked on was designed to set us up for scalability. We got serious. There were times when we asked each other really basic questions, but didn't have the information to respond. It was kind of scary actually. For example, Nick asked how much it costs to onboard a client, and we had no idea. We wanted to have the data and be able to answer any type of question about the business.

We both rolled up our sleeves and dove back into the nitty-gritty of the business. Nick spent most of his time in July working with the developers to set up our internal databases to ensure we collected all the data we needed. He ran SQL and Python scripts to crunch the numbers so we could make objective decisions. He was doing a large portion of the scripting and coding himself, which not only saved money upfront but also allowed him to use his eight years as a data scientist and algorithmic trader to play to his strengths.

In June, our churn rate was over 11 percent, so Ari got on the phone with inactive clients to see what we could do to help. More often than not, he was able to get them back on track. We calculated a valuable metric that gave us information to act on. It proved to be very worthwhile. By mid-July, our churn rate was below 3 percent, so we resumed running Facebook ads.

We also improved the onboarding process to get people engaged immediately with the service. This meant we spent more time on the phone with them upfront. We circled back to clients who signed up in the early months to re-onboard them and make sure they were aware of all of our latest capabilities and improvements. This practice was well received and helped to strengthen client relationships. We also set up automations that pinged us when someone was inactive for over a week, so we could step in and keep them active before they went dark.

In another cost saving initiative, Ari turned his attention to some of the marketing endeavors such as the podcasts and the newsletters. In fact, he started writing the newsletter himself, instead of paying a copywriter to do it. We sent out two weekly newsletters: one to the VA clients and one to a general mailing list with about eleven thousand subscribers.

He experimented with formatting and sent the newsletters from his own e-mail address, so it looked like direct, personal correspondence. For the first time in our history, the open rate climbed to 50 percent, which is very high. Not only were we saving money, but it was also an opportunity for Ari to get back into original writing, which is something he enjoys doing very much. If we hadn't been examining the analytics, we wouldn't have made the change.

Another one of Ari's goals during this time was to get himself featured as a guest on influencer podcasts to widen our reach. He had taken a year off from public speaking, but he started looking for appropriate opportunities for the fall.

In July, Nick was focused primarily on cost efficiency and scalability. His role was to manage the developers and do coding for the analytics. He's always taken a long-term view for the business and anticipated investments that would pay off in the long run. He continued his focus on improving the dashboard and automating internal processes. The VA feedback led to tweaks and changes that improved efficiencies and functionality. They were able to manage their tasks and communicate more efficiently.

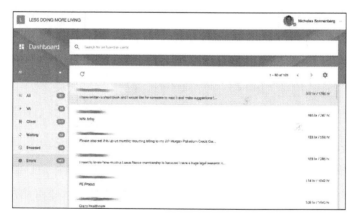

The dashboard evolved into a beautiful interface that looked a lot like e-mail, which was a completely new and innovative way to approach project management. Nick bought the template on ThemeForest for $29 and customized it for our needs. It wasn't quite ready for clients, but it was getting very close.

In the meantime, Ari concentrated on revenue generation and short-term, immediate ROI. He hustled to make sure the clients were using the services, that they were happy, and that the internal team knew what they were doing. In that vein, he wanted to change the VA onboarding process to make it more structured.

We implemented a testing battery from a company called HireSelect that could put a number score to a candidate's ability to perform the duties required of them. It even assessed their expected level of pride in their work. We wanted to bring new hires on board in groups. Training together gave them a better foundation and built a team mentality.

In the past, we'd enjoyed a more Wild West approach, but with a bigger team and increased responsibilities, we wanted to set everyone up to succeed. Plus, group training feeds into the Less Doing philosophy of batching tasks. It was far more efficient for a manager to train a handful of people instead of one-on-one.

Because of the analytics, Nick was able to identify client issues and feed them to Ari to solve. We gravitated toward the areas of the business where we thrived. Nick was happy to code for six hours and work on long-term strategies, while Ari put himself directly in front of the customers.

Nick's focus on making sure all of the tech features were fully optimized allowed us to do more with less and to be more proactive. If we suddenly got one hundred new clients overnight, we'd be ready. One of the tools that was invaluable for customer engagement was Intercom, the website chat platform. At the time, we had a two-step sign-up process on the site—a problem Nick was working on fixing. Potential clients plugged in their basic information on the first page, but by the time they clicked over to the second page to plug in their credit card information, they got cold feet. This scenario is called an abandoned cart. Whenever someone signed up for the service but didn't complete registration, a notification was sent to Ari. Within minutes, he called the person and was able to address the issue. They were always impressed to hear from one of the company founders directly. Most of them moved forward with the registration process immediately.

For Ari, it was like a hit of dopamine every time he got someone to convert. As much as Nick loved coding and building the back end, Ari loved being the front man, talking to clients, and making them feel supported. We were leveraging our unique abilities more and more.

In addition to saving dollars, our personal involvement was valuable on a deeper level. The truth is no one can do what Nick does as well as he does, and the same goes for Ari. We are uniquely qualified to handle the tasks we've assigned ourselves. This is important, because it's at the very heart of our theory of optimization. Yes, we could outsource coding and marketing and sales, and in many cases, we do, but the activities we focused on were completely in line with our unique abilities. We removed, automated, or outsourced everything else so that we could accomplish more.

Beyond focusing on quantifiable metrics, we started to meet regularly with each other. For almost a year, we'd been very casual in this regard. We hadn't had a formal review of who should be responsible for what since the very beginning. It had been a long time since we sat down to look at where we were and how our roles had changed. Given the growth and expansion of the company, it became important for us to take ownership over specific areas of the business and not just assume everything was taken care of.

We implemented a weekly meeting to check in with each other and review outstanding projects. It gave us accountability and helped us to refocus. Once we got in a groove with the meeting, we realized how remarkable it that we hadn't had a formal sit-down for ten months, especially in light of how dramatically our responsibilities had changed.

SOLUTIONS

When we first hired Brit to help us with some Chargify implementations, we thought we just needed a little help here and there, but it seemed like every day we needed something urgent taken care of. He quickly became indispensable. It was Brit's idea to implement Intercom and another tool called Segment, which is a customer data hub. As much as we needed him, his hours were stacking up. Our freelance developer, Jeff, was working on the dashboard full time too. Between the two of them, we were spending about $8,000/month, plus $12,000 on additional internal improvements.

We had always talked about introducing some sort of equity share for our top performers. In July, after speaking with our accountant and lawyer, we came up with a more concrete plan for Brit, Casey, Alana, and Florence. They had always demonstrated devotion and efficiency in their work, but when we rolled out an equity share plan, we saw a dramatic overnight shift in productivity. They started to think strategically, which was a game changer. With owner stake, we trusted them to consistently make the best decisions for the business.

We made our numbers transparent to the stakeholders and gave them access to Chart Mogul. We felt it was important for them to be able to see that they were vested in something real, with consistent, measurable growth. Offering our key staff an incentive to stick around was one of the best decisions we made.

There were additional simplifications that helped make the company function more smoothly. For referrals, we offered a 10 percent discount on monthly subscription fee for as long as they were a client, regardless of who made the introduction. We simplified the discount on purchasing hours. Anyone who purchased over forty hours at a time was eligible for a 5 percent discount.

We decided not to take out a credit line or raise money. We forced ourselves to dig ourselves out of the financial hole, which meant we had to get creative. We introduced an annual discount plan. We talked it over and thought it was great way to raise some quick cash and incentivize new subscribers. We had several marketing initiatives lined up for October, and an annual plan for $1,200 was a nice option to offer. We sent an e-mail to all of our existing clients announcing the new plan, and a handful of people signed up immediately. It was exactly the quick cash injection we needed at the time. In addition, Ari was in his third year of certifying Less Doing Coaches. We combined our knowledge to offer the coaches all that we had learned through a yearlong mastermind program. A single e-mail to our list resulted in five high-ticket sales, not to mention a new group of future Less Doing ambassadors.

The month got off to a rocky start, but because of our hustle and the vast improvements we made to virtually every section of the business, July was our best month ever. We broke the $100,000 mark, reduced the number of VA internal hours from 42 percent to 34 percent, and began concentrating exclusively in the areas where we personally excelled. By employing the processes of optimizing, automating, and outsourcing, our own business has been streamlined to be the most effective and productive version of itself possible. In building the company over the course of twelve months, we evolved to embody our own core philosophy.

CONCLUSION

We're often asked what we would do differently if we had it all to do again. Hindsight is always twenty-twenty, but we're happy to say there aren't too many things we'd change. Of course, we've learned some valuable lessons and approached problems in a new way.

A year ago, we thought we were in the business of virtual assistants, but we realized we were really in the business of making companies more efficient. We didn't initially offer subscriptions, and we didn't immediately think of ourselves as a total solutions provider. As the year unfolded and we grew, we evolved into a sleek and highly efficient ally for businesses and individuals. That's truly how we see ourselves. We were invested in our clients' success as much, if not more than, our own. Our highly trained VAs and team of specialists can handle any task or project that comes their way.

With zero investment dollars, we've bootstrapped our way to profitability by always looking for better ways to do what we're doing. We were forced to be resourceful and maximize our time and dollars because we didn't have either to put into the business.

Over time, we learned to make objective, data-driven decisions, rather than fly by the seat of our pants through continual experimentation. We pushed ourselves and each other to the degree that we were able to ask tough questions and have hard conversations when necessary. The level of trust and respect we share for one another is one of the key contributors to our continued growth and enduring strength.

Optimize, automate, and outsource is a journey. Without this mind-set, we wouldn't have been able to function at the same level from day one, or grow the business in the way we have. You have to go through the motions, which is why at the beginning we were looking at all of the VAs' tasks, managing payroll, and getting our hands dirty with the details. As we evolved, we've been able to off-load the activities that are executed more efficiently by other people or systems. You can't progress or grow if you focus on the same tasks day in and day out.

Throughout the life of the company, we've constantly been

flexible and adaptive, almost on a daily basis. The original hypothesis, and the genesis of the business, was about testing and validating ideas. We've taken it to another level. By consistently reinvesting in the company, we chose to take a long-term view instead of concentrating on immediate returns. We've leveraged free technology tools to make the company scalable and sustainable from day one.

Through the proper allocation of people, time, money, and tools, we have been able to grow strategically. We are constantly optimizing where we are investing our resources to make sure we are always making the most impact. We are far from perfect. There's always room for improvement. Every day, we try to be better, stronger, faster, and smarter, and will continue to do so as long as we're in business.

RESOURCES

TECH

1Password [password management] 1password.com

ActiveCampaign [e-mail marketing] www.activecampaign.com

Asana [project management software] asana.com

Blue Fish [high-end concierge service] thebluefish.com

Book In A Box [ghostwriting] bookinabox.com

Calendly [scheduling tool] www.calendly.com

Calvin [smart planning tool] www.calvinapp.com

Chargify [billing portal] www.chargify.com

ChartMogul [financial dashboard] chartmogul.com

Checkr [background checks] checkr.com

ClickFunnels [analytics for sales funnels] www.clickfunnels.com

DropBox [cloud storage] dropbox.com

DropVox [voice recorder] itunes.apple.com/us/app/dropvox-record-voice-memos/id416288287?mt=8

Evernote [virtual notebook] evernote.com

Fancy Hands [on-demand virtual assistants] www.fancyhands.com

Front [shared team inbox] frontapp.com

HelloSign [electronic signatures] www.hellosign.com

HireSelect [pre-employment testing] www.criteriacorp.com/index_alt.php

IFTTT [automation tool] www.ifttt.com

Intercom [marketing tool for communicating with customers] www.intercom.io

Intuit Workforce [hiring management] workforce.intuit.com

LastPass [password storing/sharing] lastpass.com

Lessonly [online quiz platform] www.lessonly.com

MailChimp [e-mail campaigns] mailchimp.com

Mode Analytics [business intelligence tool] modeanalytics.com

Rocket Lawyer [on-demand legal help] www.rocketlawyer.com

Roger [asynchronous communication] rogertalk.com

Schedule Once [scheduling tool] www.scheduleonce.com

Skype [web conferencing] www.skype.com

Slack [team communication tool] www.slack.com

Smooch [chat with customers on your website] smooch.io

Stripe [payment processing] www.stripe.com

Sway [slackbot for finances] swayfinance.com

ThemeForest [website templates for sale] themeforest.net

Toggl [time tracking] www.toggl.com

Trello [project/task management tool] www.trello.com

Twilio [programmable sms] www.twilio.com

Wistia [video marketing platform] wistia.com

YouTube [video storage platform] www.youtube.com

Zirtual [dedicated virtual assistants] www.zirtual.com

Zoom [web conferencing] www.zoom.us

PEOPLE

Jay Abraham: CEO, The Abraham Group, www.abraham.co

Andre Chaperon: Internet Marketer, Entrepreneur, andrechaperon.com

Sarah Clasing: Cofounder, Hinge Analytics, hingeanalytics.com

Nir Eyal: Author of Hooked, www.nirandfar.com

Jonathon Keidan: Cofounder, Inside Hook, www.insidehook.com

Nathan Latka: Entreprenuer, nathanlatka.com

Jonathan Levy: Behavioral Scientist, www.jonlevytlb.com

Nico Marsiglia: Systemik Solutions, www.systemiksolutions.com

Joe Polish: Founder, Genius Network, geniusnetwork.com and

    Cofounder, Ilovemarketing podcast, ilovemarketing.com

Sue Rice: CEO, Slice International, slice.international/about-sue

Taly Russell: CEO, SilverChair Partners, www.silverchairpartners.com

Aaron Schiff: CEO, Matic Insurance, maticinsurance.com

INTERESTING CLIENT TASKS FROM OUR FIRST YEAR

- Created an automated system to publish weekly pod-casts and post to social media using Zapier, Rev, and Trello
- Created an automated system to fulfill supplement orders using Squarespace ecommerce and Trello
- Created and published an e-book into a hard copy for a client
- Provided local knowledge of Rome for an off-the-beaten-track weekend
- Helped a client relocate with her four children, including looking after visas, temporary accommodation, health care, and removalists

- Created a brochure advertisement that was used in the 2015 Oscars—the eighty-seventh Academy Awards
- Created Less Doing's first sales funnel to automate the sales of the VA service
- Automated social media postings so that we didn't have to touch it for two months
- Found tickets to a sold-out museum opening
- Helped a client reach Inbox Zero (from Inbox 3,000+)
- Created an infographic to be used as a snapshot to track personal finances
- Created a podcast from the ground up, including the bumpers, artwork, and social media campaign, as well as producing the audio
- Published a music album to an international audience online, including services such as Apple Music, Google Play, and Spotify
- Researched and ordered numerous parts for a complete car customization to allow for a comfier, quieter, and more stylish car
- Wrote an e-book on soccer coachingCreated a series of eighty-one photos with inspirational quotes and then scheduled them to be posted on social media
- Found a wash and fold service in Nuremberg, Germany, and set up a regular washing pickup and delivery (with the non-English-speaking service provider)
- Interviewed Sally Hogshead's entire team to understand their processes and to document their individual

responsibilities in order to simplify their work

- Built a sales funnel from scratch for a wealth/asset management and financial counselor
- Created a custom fitness and meal plan for a client who wanted to be healthier, but didn't have much time for those activities
- Researched an anniversary gift for a client's wife
- Helped a client develop a course that will become a program he can sell
- Collected over $10,000 in past due payments for a law firm
- Developed a twenty-nine-page, nine-thousand-word market analysis on the country of Belize that included twenty-five hours of formal academic research
- Created a three- to six-month blogger outreach strategy prior to an Indiegogo crowdfunding campaign to organically grow backers
- Sold a car on eBay
- Found twelve hundred heart-shaped chocolates and got free delivery in less than twenty-four hours
- Set up a video recording page to collect video testimonials
- Assisted the transition of a physical company office into a virtual office
- Found a house inspector to come out on a Friday (on a holiday weekend) with a couple of days' notice
- Brainstormed names for a speaking event involving

finances and the 2016 presidential election

- Found a small travel case for a single essential oil bottle— which was more difficult than you might think
- Hired an office assistant to come into a client's office in Miami and spend two days organizing it
- Upgraded an entire website from scratch, which included transferring it to another domain
- Rewrote a client's bio in three ways for three different platforms
- Assisted in the market research and writing of a grant application for $100,000 in funding
- Helped arrange food and shelter for our client's client, who happens to be homeless and schizophrenic
- Planned five unforgettable dates and weekend get- aways for a client and his girlfriend (exotic animals, swimming with sharks/dolphins, fancy dinners, etc.)
- Found the best lease for a four-door sedan, with the client looking to spend $300 per month and $3000 down, with the most modern tech, safety, and drivability such as a BMW 3 series or Mercedes C class

ACKNOWLEDGMENTS

———

Ari would like to acknowledge his wife, Anna, and his four children: Benjamin, Sébastien, Lucas, and Chloe. Nick would like to thank his girlfriend, Francesca, for all of her incredible support through this adventure.

We would both like to recognize the entire team at Less Doing Virtual Assistants for all of their efforts in making this venture what it is today. Thank you Florence, Alana, Casey P., Agnes, Andrew, Casey F., Charles, Chris, Dan, Ike, Luke, Heidi, Jess F., Jess B., Joe, Kelly, Laura, Lauren, Matt, Mike, Rachel, Ross, Tanya, Tim, Will, Raenelle, Jeff, Micala, and Brit.

So many wonderful people provided feedback on the book (yes, we outsourced a bit of the editing): Case Larsen, Claire Hobson, Blake Eastman, Casey Pennington, Linda

Kreitzman, Eric Wakkuri, Rachel Bell, Paula Abreu, Guilherme Nunes, Anupam Mathur, Jeff Madoff, Heidi Krupp, and Kassandra Kuehl.

This book wouldn't have been possible without the help of some key mentors. Joe Polish has been an incredible friend and partner. His generosity and marketing genius has been instrumental in our success so far. Jay Abraham, for his incredible advice and support in the beginning stages of our journey. Jeff Madoff, for his branding help and advice on the book title.

Thank you to all of our clients who believed in our service, patronized us, and helped make us better every day. We definitely wouldn't be here without you

And it would have been impossible to tell this story without our editor, Brooke White.

ABOUT THE AUTHORS

NICK SONNENBERG is a serial entrepreneur with a passion for numbers. After graduating from UC Berkeley with a master's in financial engineering, Nick worked on Wall Street for eight years as a high-frequency algorithmic trader.

By twenty-seven, he was managing a multibillion-dollar stock portfolio. His responsibilities included creating algorithms and writing computer programs to analyze the algorithms' performance. The computer traded billions of dollars in stocks at microsecond speeds to capture fractions of a penny. Nick's job was to understand where money was being made or lost and constantly analyze the algorithms to maximize profits. Although he was successful, Nick was unfulfilled and anxious to lead a more meaningful life.

He took a leap into the entrepreneurial space to focus on his passion for productivity. He wanted to leverage his quantitative abilities to solve real-world business problems. He created a productivity app, called Calvin, which was an innovative way for people to make plans with each other. Through trading and Calvin, Nick developed a deep respect for entrepreneurship and an appreciation for automation and data science.

His fascination with optimization and automation in business has led him to his latest project, Less Doing, where he is able to apply a systematic and quantitative approach to all aspects of the company. In his free time, you can find him spending time with his girlfriend while playing speed chess in Washington Square Park.

ARI MEISEL'S story starts in 2006, when some unexpected news derailed his booming real estate career: Crohn's Disease. A highly debilitating digestive ailment, Crohn's barred Ari from leading a normal life. He lost weight, energy, and the ability to work with regularity—in fact, there were times he could only work for sixty minutes a day.

With a blossoming business to run, Ari knew an hour per day wasn't going to lead to success. Against the advice of doctors and loved ones, Ari embarked upon an extraordinarily painful journey to cure what medical textbooks consider an incurable disease.

Through excruciating amounts of trial and error, Ari not only regained control of his life but also beat this seemingly unbeatable disease and is now symptom-free.

Less Doing, More Living; Less Doing Virtual Assistants; and Less Doing BPO (Business Process Optimization) are the result of Ari's amazing journey back to health, happiness, and well-being. Ari currently lives in New York City, where he spends every ounce of free time with his family.

IT'S TIME TO WRITE YOUR BOOK

———

"People kept telling me 'You should really write another book.' I wanted to, but I couldn't. I tried a few times, but I just couldn't make it come out of me. Book In A Box was just the perfect solution to the problems I was having."

— ARI MEISEL

Ari was struggling with something a lot of writers struggle with. He knew the concepts he wanted in his book, and he knew his material cold, but he was so deep in the weeds (and strapped for time) that he couldn't get the perspective he needed to write the book he wanted to write.

It was only through his conversations with the professional publishing team at Book In A Box that Ari was able to create the exact book he wanted and then launch that book in the world in the way he knew would work best for him.

Book In A Box is a company that turns ideas into books.

We surround our authors with a team of publishing professionals who help clarify and structure their book idea, get their words out of their head (in their voice), and then professionally publish their book in about ten times less time than if they do it themselves.

Ari and Nick used us for the book you have in your hands, and Ari used us for his last book, *The Art of Less Doing*.

If you have valuable ideas in your head as well and believe they might make a good book, we're happy to talk and see if we can help.

Start here: www.bookinabox.com/lessdoing